COVID-19 AND TRANSPORT IN ASIA AND THE PACIFIC

GUIDANCE NOTE

DECEMBER 2020

ADB

ASIAN DEVELOPMENT BANK

© 2020 Asian Development Bank
6 ADB Avenue, Mandaluyong City, 1550 Metro Manila, Philippines
Tel +63 2 8632 4444; Fax +63 2 8636 2444
www.adb.org

Some rights reserved. Published in 2020.

ISBN 978-92-9262-582-5 (print); 978-92-9262-583-2 (electronic); 978-92-9262-584-9 (ebook)
Publication Stock No. TIM200398
DOI: http://dx.doi.org/10.22617/TIM200398

Notes:
In this publication, "$" refers to United States dollars unless otherwise stated.
ADB recognizes "Hong Kong" as Hong Kong, China; "China" as the People's Republic of China; and "Korea" as the Republic of Korea.

On the cover: The transport sector faces challenges due to restrictions and lockdowns implemented to cope with the coronavirus disease (COVID-19). The impact of the pandemic is evident across the globe (photos by Veejay Villafranca, Afriadi Hikmal, Narendra Shrestha, Richard Atrero de Guzman and Richard Atrero de Guzman for ADB).

Cover design by Anthony Villanueva.

Contents

Tables, Figures, and Boxes

Tables

Figures

Boxes

Acknowledgments

The Asian Development Bank wishes to acknowledge the valuable inputs and contributions of all stakeholders that contributed to this publication. The preparation of this guidance note was led by Jamie Leather, chief of Transport Sector Group Secretariat under the Sustainable Development and Climate Change Department. Robert Guild, chief sector officer, provided support and overall guidance. Inputs were sourced from Ki-Joon Kim (principal transport specialist), Robert Valkovic (principal transport specialist), Michael Anyala (senior road asset management specialist), Alexandra Pamela Chiang (senior transport specialist), Kuancheng Huang (senior transport specialist), and Diana Hernandez-Louis (transport officer). Independent expert consultants Cornie Huizenga and Sudhir Gota supported with technical analyses. The production of the publication was managed by Franzella "Pinky" Villanueva (associate operations analyst), Noel Chavez (operations assistant), and Andres Kawagi Fernan (communications consultant).

This guidance note is part of a sector-specific series by the Asian Development Bank in response to the coronavirus disease (COVID-19), under the direction of Woochong Um of the Sustainable Development and Climate Change Department.

Abbreviations

ADB	Asian Development Bank
CO_2	carbon dioxide
COVID-19	coronavirus disease
DMC	developing member country
EU	European Union
GDP	gross domestic product
IATA	International Air Transport Association
NO_2	nitrogen dioxide
PM	particulate matter
PRC	People's Republic of China
Q	quarter
RPK	revenue passenger kilometer
US	United States

Executive Summary

The spread of the coronavirus disease (COVID-19) since the beginning of 2020 has been dramatic in terms of its speed, scale, and economic and social impact. The highly interconnected nature of 21st century globalization allowed the virus to reach nearly all corners of the globe within a few months. Successive lockdowns around the world have caused a sharp decline in global demand and supply of goods and services. As cities and countries contemplate reopening, the foremost challenge governments face is how to balance the health of the population with that of the economy.

Transport has played a central role in the spread of the virus. It has also played a critical part in enabling frontline and essential workers to get to work during the pandemic, and will continue to represent an enabler in terms of supporting the different needs of the population throughout the different stages of recovery. The pandemic's impact on passenger and freight transport has been profound. Mobility restrictions in response to COVID-19 have resulted in drastic changes in travel behavior (Figure E1). Swift lockdowns across the globe forced all nonessential workers to work from home almost overnight, and schools to shift to e-learning. With the closure of brick-and-mortar shops and restaurants during the containment period, consumers flocked to online shopping and food delivery. The sharp reductions in economic activity have also curbed regional and national freight transport activity. On the other hand, in many places, urban freight and logistics have prospered as a result of increased online shopping and food deliveries.

The overall picture that emerges is one of a sharp decline in transport activity after lockdowns or other forms of restrictions were imposed in the second half of the first quarter of 2020. Transport activity bottomed between mid-April and mid-May. After this, following a relaxation of restrictions, a gradual return to pre-COVID-19 levels can be observed, either because the virus had been brought under control or because governments argued that, even though it had not, they had no choice but to reopen the economy.

Concerns over close physical contact have also affected the perceived quality and attractiveness of different travel mode choices. While previous perceptions may have been that public transit was an efficient and affordable mode of travel, initial trends in cities that have reopened indicate that public transit is still considered unsafe relative to the use of private vehicles, cycling, and walking, and is not bouncing back as quickly.

While a rebound to old ways of working, learning, and leisure may occur post-containment, it is also quite likely that a new norm will emerge, with increased uptake of these private modes of transport compared with pre-pandemic times. Such new behaviors could change trip patterns across the different travel purposes. With a return to pre-pandemic transport activity levels, reductions in air pollution, carbon dioxide emissions, and road accidents may well come to represent a temporary phenomenon.

Figure E1: Impact of COVID-19 on Transport in Asia and the Pacific

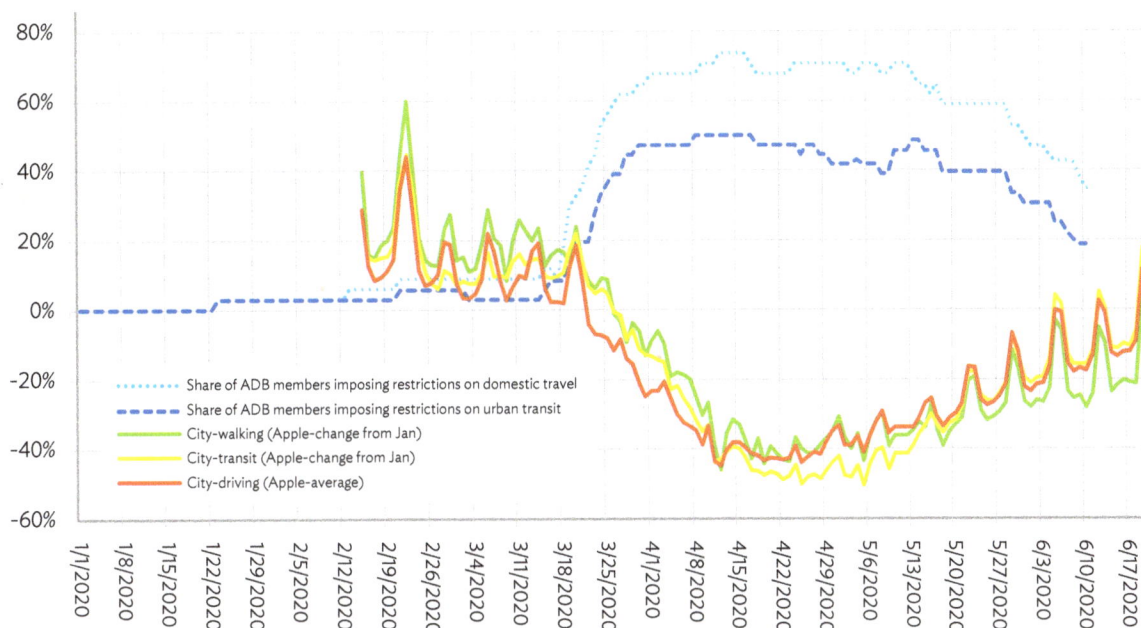

Legend:
- Share of ADB members imposing restrictions on domestic travel
- Share of ADB members imposing restrictions on urban transit
- City-walking (Apple-change from Jan)
- City-transit (Apple-change from Jan)
- City-driving (Apple-average)

ADB = Asian Development Bank, COVID-19 = coronavirus disease.
Sources: University of Oxford. Coronavirus Government Response Tracker (accessed 24 June 2020); Google. COVID-19 Community Mobility Reports (accessed 24 June 2020); and Apple Inc. Mobility Trends Reports (accessed 24 June 2020).

Some governments have launched financial stimulus measures in response to the COVID-19 pandemic. The transport sector is benefiting from these through financial support to the airline industry, the automotive sector, and public transit companies. Within the global transport community, a range of good practices is being developed to which policy makers, regulators, and especially transport operators in Asia can refer to enhance the health resilience of transport systems and reduce the likelihood of infections of users as lockdowns are eased.

A "bounce-back strategy and framework" has been developed for each transport subsector to assist countries exiting lockdowns (Figure 20). The strategy covers three phases: the response phase in the immediate term (up to 3 months), the recovery phase in the medium term (up to 1 year), and rejuvenation in the longer term (after 1 year). In the case of repeated waves of transmissions, countries may fall back to earlier phases midway through the recovery and repeat the successive phases in the three-stage process. This is a stylized strategy; it is important to be aware that the actual response will vary between countries and cities, and between different transport subsectors within countries and cities.

In the response phase, travel is still expected to be limited, with the focus mainly on allowing essential workers to travel and enabling the shipment of goods. Measures include protecting transport staff and passengers, as well as frequent cleaning and sanitization. Complementing these, a robust system of contact tracing and health monitoring needs to be put in place.

In the recovery phase, travel restrictions are relaxed. For cargo movement, streamlined measures are implemented, such as the establishment of dedicated lanes for freight vehicles and coordinated travel documentation requirements across borders to remove duplicative processes. For passenger movement, systems gradually open up with enhanced sanitation, face mask protection, thermal scanning, and tracing measures. Many urban transport systems are relaxing social distancing measures to ensure sufficient capacity.

In the rejuvenation phase, further preventive and precautionary operating measures are introduced, together with advanced technology, to enable contactless processes and facilitate an agile response. As a complementary measure, capacity for walking and cycling could be scaled up to accommodate people who would normally have taken public transport. To cope with lower and uncertain travel demand on public transit, aviation, and certain strategic freight routes, it is critical to assess if restructuring or subsidies for concessions or service agreements are required to keep essential transport links open and ensure core transport and freight operators remain financially viable.

Regardless of the COVID-19 pandemic, it is clear that developing Asia and the Pacific will continue to have a substantial need for additional transport infrastructure and services. Therefore, there will be a continued demand for multilateral development banks, such as the Asian Development Bank (ADB), to play an important role in the development of transport infrastructure and services in Asia. Not all of the transport operations supported by ADB are equally sensitive to COVID-19, during the development and implementation phase or in their subsequent operation. National, urban, and rural road-based projects can largely proceed as planned, with precautions built in for workers, especially during the construction phase. Urban public transport projects are likely to be the most sensitive, given uncertainty related to future usage and the length and intensity of the pandemic.

Technological advances, big data, artificial intelligence, digitalization, and automation, combined with behavioral change that prioritizes more sustainable transport options, offer fresh innovative solutions to the development of the transport sector. Enhanced efforts in such areas can help realize the Sustainable Development Goals and the Paris Agreement while considering the lessons of COVID-19 pandemic, which has highlighted the need for a more robust transport system that is "green" and resilient to future disasters.

1 Introduction and Purpose of the Guidance Note

The coronavirus disease (COVID-19) outbreak began in the city of Wuhan, People's Republic of China (PRC), in late 2019. By the turn of 2020, the virus had spread rapidly to members of the Asian Development Bank (ADB) in East Asia and Southeast Asia, such as Hong Kong, China; Japan; the Republic of Korea; Singapore; Taipei,China; and Thailand. Thereafter, it found its way further afield such as Australia, the European Union (EU), and the United States (US) (Figure 1). By June 2020, the overall number of cases in Asia showed an upward trend, with most of the growth taking place in South Asia, while infection numbers in East Asia, which peaked in the first quarter (Q1) of 2020, were stabilizing at a relatively low level.

Alarmed by the speed of transmission and the severity of the illness, on 11 March 2020, the World Health Organization declared the COVID-19 outbreak a global pandemic. A range of interventions were implemented across the world, including in various Asian countries, to reduce contact and physical interaction among individuals to slow down and break the chain of transmission. These included safe distancing, a stricter disinfection and sanitization regime of public spaces and personal hygiene, and lockdowns.[1]

---

1 East Asian countries the PRC, the Republic of Korea, and Viet Nam were the first to implement widespread containment measures, with Africa, much of Europe, Latin America, and North America taking longer to bring in tough restrictions. (*Financial Times*. 2020. Exiting Lockdowns: Tracking Governments' Changing Coronavirus Responses. 15 July.)

Figure 1: COVID-19 Transmission, 2020
(number of cases, millions)

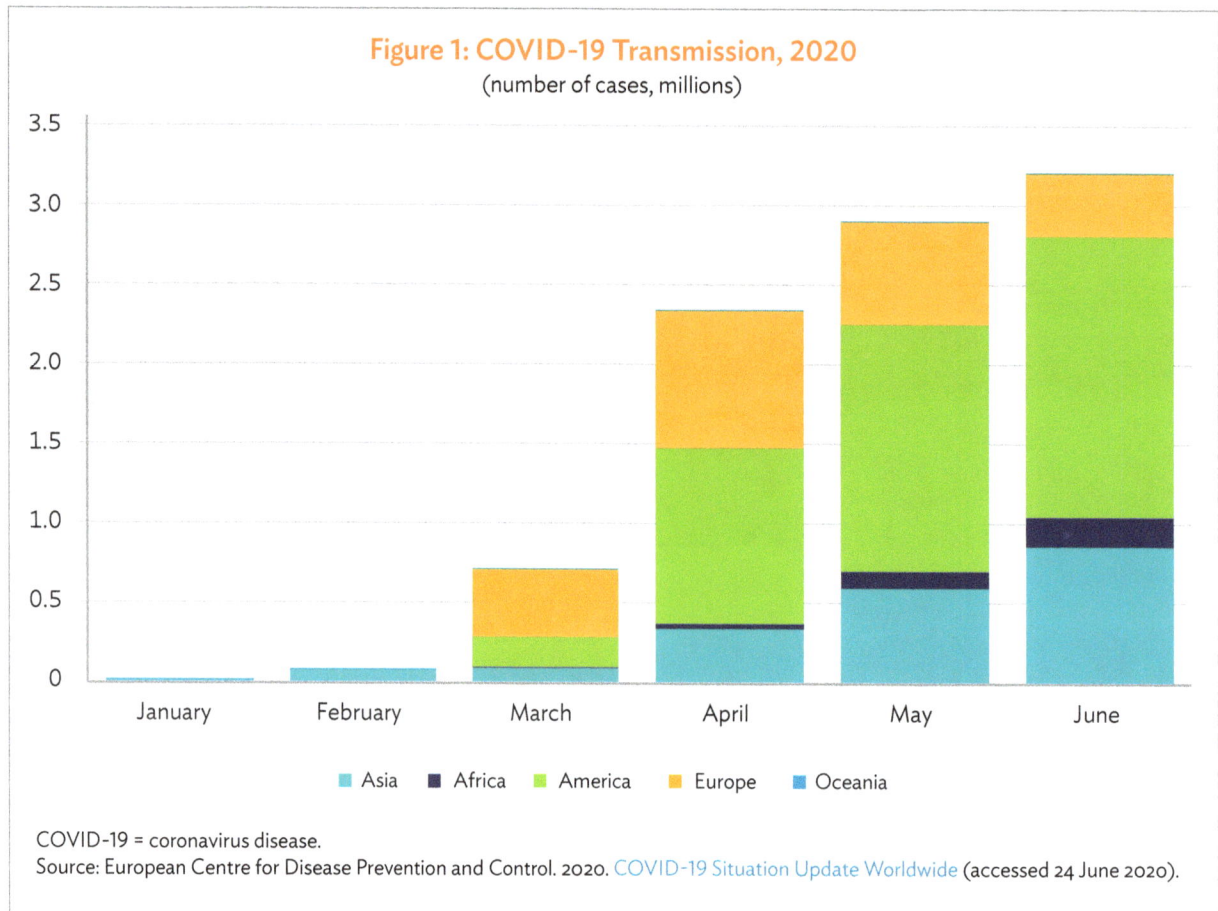

COVID-19 = coronavirus disease.
Source: European Centre for Disease Prevention and Control. 2020. COVID-19 Situation Update Worldwide (accessed 24 June 2020).

Transport is playing a key role in the spread of COVID-19 both through international and domestic travel (Box 1). In ADB's developing member countries (DMCs), the first suspensions of public transit, buses, railways, flights, and ferry services were seen in the PRC on 23 January 2020 in the cities of Ezhou, Huanggang, and Wuhan. Initially, other countries restricted flights from the PRC or from countries with large numbers of reported cases. Thereafter, restrictions were also imposed throughout Asia, in specific cities or nationwide, across other modes— road, rail, and sea. These local and international travel restrictions resulted in a ban on almost all international travel and a ban or restrictions on much of domestic travel. By the middle of June 2020, 194 countries had implemented full or partial lockdown.[2] Most International travel was restricted, except for humanitarian, logistical, and diplomatic purposes.[3]

The PRC, including the city of Wuhan, reopened for business in April, more than 70 days after it locked down on 23 January 2020. An easing of restrictions in other Asian countries (Japan, Malaysia, and Viet Nam) followed shortly thereafter. Affected countries around the world and in Asia are anxious to relax restrictions and reboot economies amid fears of the worst economic recession since the Great Depression of the 1930s.[4] However, many countries are taking a cautious approach to relaxing their early stringent measures of restricting the movement

[2]   K. Lee et al. 2020. Global Coordination on Cross-Border Travel and Trade Measures Crucial to COVID-19 Response. *The Lancet.* 395 (10237). pp. 1593–1595.
[3]   D. Dunford et al. 2020. Coronavirus: The World in Lockdown in Maps and Charts. *BBC News.* 6 April.
[4]   G. Gopinath. 2020. Reopening from the Great Lockdown: Uneven and Uncertain Recovery. *IMFBlog: Insights & Analysis on Economics & Finance.* 24 June.

BOX 1

Evidence on the Role of Transport in the Spread of COVID-19

Yahua Zhang et al. have found that the frequencies of air flights and high-speed train services out of Wuhan were significantly associated with the number of coronavirus disease (COVID-19) cases in the destination cities. (Y. Zhang et al. 2020. Exploring the Roles of High-Speed Train, Air and Coach Services in the Spread of COVID-19 in China. *Transport Policy*. 94. pp. 34–42.)

Ruizhi Zheng et al. have found a significant and positive association between the frequency of flights, trains, and buses from Wuhan and the daily and cumulative numbers of COVID-19 cases in other cities, with progressively increased correlations for public transit. The distance between Wuhan and other cities was inversely associated with the numbers of COVID-19 cases in that city (all P values < 0.001), and the correlation became increasingly strong and became stable after 1 February 2020. (R. Zheng et al. 2020. Spatial Transmission of COVID-19 via Public and Private Transportation in China. *Travel Medicine and Infectious Disease*. 34. p. 101626.)

Darlan S. Candido et al. have established the role of within- and between-state mobility as a key driver of both local and interregional virus spread, with highly populated and well-connected urban municipalities acting as main sources of virus exports within Brazil. (D. Candido et al. 2020. Evolution and Epidemic Spread of SARS-CoV-2 in Brazil. *Science*. 369 (6508). pp. 1255–1260.)

Hien Lau et al. have found a strong linear correlation between domestic COVID-19 cases and passenger volume for regions within the People's Republic of China and a significant relationship between international COVID-19 cases and passenger volume. (H. Lau et al. 2020. The Association between International and Domestic Air Traffic and the Coronavirus (COVID-19) Outbreak. *Journal of Microbiology, Immunology and Infection*. 53 (3). pp. 467–472.)

Research from the University of California, Berkeley, has found that home isolation, business closures, and lockdowns have often produced the clearest benefits. Travel restrictions and bans on gatherings have had mixed results, with large effects in some countries—France and Iran, for example—and less clear benefits in countries such as the United States. (S. Hsang et al. 2020. The Effect of Large-Scale Anti-Contagion Policies on the COVID-19 Pandemic. *Nature*. 584. pp. 262–267.)

Kelley Lee et al. have established that global coordination on cross-border travel and trade measures is crucial to the COVID-19 response. (K. Lee et al. 2020. Global Coordination on Cross-Border Travel and Trade Measures Crucial to COVID-19 Response. *The Lancet*. 395. pp. 1593–1595.)

Source: Compiled by the Asian Development Bank.

---

of their populations, and hoping that a second wave of infection will not occur. Other countries, or regions and cities, have argued that economic considerations are more important than health considerations and have started opening up even though key COVID-19-related indicators are still well above values recommended by the World Health Organization.

The purpose of this guidance note is to share (i) collective experiences on how COVID-19 is affecting social and travel behaviors in Asia and the Pacific and how the transport sector is responding in the face of the crisis and (ii) guiding principles and good practices in transport operations to support economic recovery. The fight against COVID-19 is expected to be long. Some experts believe COVID-19 may not be wiped out completely until a vaccine is developed and disseminated widely. In the meantime, new solutions are required to enhance the resilience of transport services and infrastructure to keep economies running and growing without compromising public health. The crisis has already inspired innovations across the sector, highlighting opportunities for future partnerships and synergies.

Insights shared in this guidance note are expected to be of relevance and interest to DMCs, the private sector, and interested stakeholders, regionally and internationally, as they deliver resilient infrastructure in the Asia and Pacific region and beyond. The guidance note also assesses the impact of COVID-19 on ADB's transport portfolio and pipeline.

Chapter 2 discusses the impact of COVID-19 on travel demand and mobility patterns in Asia, Chapter 3 discusses the role of transport in exit strategies from COVID-19 restrictions, and Chapter 4 concludes by offering a glimpse of what the future could hold for transport after COVID-19. The appendixes provide further information, such as a timeline of transport and mobility restrictions in various economies, detailed bounce-back measures for each subsector, and other useful guidelines and references.

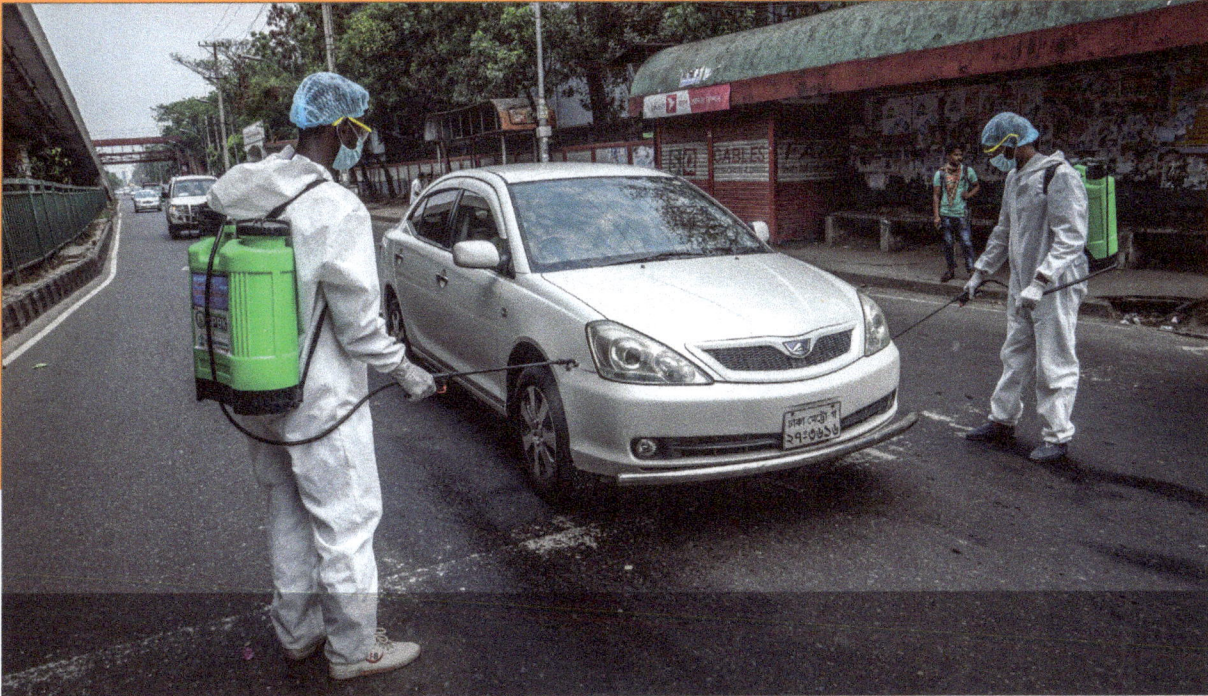

2 How COVID-19 is Changing Travel Demand and Mobility Patterns in Asia

Toward the end of Q1 2020 and at the beginning of Q2 2020, governments around the world, including in Asia, imposed large-scale stay-at-home and quarantine notices and implemented swift measures to move work and schools online, close recreational venues and public places, and ban large-scale events and gatherings. An overwhelming majority of economies have been affected, regardless of the extent to which restrictive measures were implemented—reflecting the high degree of interdependence among countries. Travel demand across all transport subsectors has fallen dramatically, with aviation the most severely affected.

Drivers of Change in Travel Demand and Mobility Patterns in Asia

The pandemic has forced all transport users to reassess the necessity of their trips and resulted in temporary new travel patterns. At this point, it is hard to predict the extent to which these new behaviors will be sustained. It is probable that, even after lockdowns are lifted, work-from-home and e-learning arrangements will still be used more frequently compared with pre-COVID-19. This could change travel behavior and patterns, including the frequency and distance of trips. Depending on the net effect on overall travel demand, this may have varying impacts on the environment through changes in traffic congestion, carbon dioxide (CO_2) emissions, and air and noise pollution.

Trade and Economy

Transport demand is derived from the level of economic activity and trade. With the unprecedented disruption to the global economy and trade, all transport subsectors are feeling the effects of COVID-19. Regional economic growth in Asia is set to decline sharply in 2020. The World Trade Organization has estimated that world merchandise trade will shrink by 13%–32% in 2020, depending on how quickly the virus is contained and trade can return to pre-crisis levels.[5]

Travel Restrictions

Table 1 gives an overview of the status of measures to restrict domestic travel, urban public transit, and international transport across ADB members on 10 June 2020. Further details on the restrictions are in Appendix 1. International transport was restricted to the largest extent, followed by urban public transit and domestic travel.

As COVID-19 spread across the globe in Q1 2020, international borders were shut at short notice in an attempt to curtail transmissions, particularly from March 2020. Most business trips were canceled or replaced by teleconferencing and other forms of digital communication. While several domestic Asian cities are lifting travel restrictions, the restoration of international flights and travel is not proceeding at the same pace. Reopening of borders in the medium term is expected to be cautious and limited. Some countries—such as Australia, Fiji, New Zealand, the PRC, and Singapore—are now considering the "travel bubble" concept, whereby air travel could take place between countries with low transmission rates, on a reciprocal basis, with controlled measures to monitor health and movement of international passengers.[6]

Figure 2 illustrates the introduction of cross-national and cross-temporal international transport policies in ADB members since the outbreak of COVID-19. On 14 June 2020, 10% of ADB members imposed quarantine laws (with screening), 35% imposed a ban on flights from high-risk regions, and 55% implemented total border closure. Initial screening of international passengers (up to the end of March 2020) was incorporated in the more restrictive quarantine measures or became irrelevant after complete border closures were imposed from late March. As of 15 June 2020, no ADB member had completely removed restrictions on international transport movement.[7]

Commuting and Working Practices

While the uptake of work-from-home practices had been patchy prior to the pandemic, the swift lockdowns across the globe forced many organizations to adopt remote work practices, as far as it was practicable, overnight, so as to maintain productivity. Face-to-face business meetings and overseas business travel have been replaced by virtual meetings. A wide range of communication and collaboration tools, such as Google Meet, Microsoft Teams, Skype, and Zoom, have enabled companies and individuals to adapt to this shift.[8]

---

5   F. Richter. 2020. The COVID-19 Economy: Does It Mean the End of Globalization? *The World Economic Forum COVID Action Platform*. 29 May.

6   L. Marcus. 2020. Fiji Plans to Create a Post-Coronavirus Travel Bubble with New Zealand and Australia. *CNN*. 22 June; and Z. Abdullah. 2020. Business and Official Travelers on Singapore-China 'Fast Lane' Arrangement Must Get COVID-19 Swab Tests. *Channel News Asia*. 3 June.

7   Detailed international transport policy measures on international aviation adopted by ADB members can be found at International Air Transport Association. COVID-19 Government Public Health Mitigation Measures.

8   Zoom's revenue in its fiscal Q1 more than doubled compared with the same period in 2019, to $328 million. *Associated Press*. 2020. Zoom Booms as Teleconferencing Company Profits from Coronavirus Crisis. 2 June.

Table 1: Overview of Restrictions on Domestic Travel, Urban Public Transit, and International Transport in Selected ADB Members

Transport COVID-19 Policy Status as of 10 June 2020			
Country	Domestic Travel	Urban Public Transit	International Transport
Australia	Require closing	None to limited measures	Total border closure
Azerbaijan	Require closing	None to limited measures	Total border closure
Bangladesh	None to limited measures	Recommended closing	Ban on high-risk region
Bhutan	Require closing	Recommended closing	Total border closure
Brunei Darussalam	Recommended closing	None to limited measures	Total border closure
Cambodia	None to limited measures	None to limited measures	Quarantine arrivals
Georgia	Recommended closing	None to limited measures	Total border closure
India	Require closing	Require closing	Ban on high-risk region
Indonesia	Recommended closing	None to limited measures	Total border closure
Japan	None to limited measures	None to limited measures	Ban on high-risk region
Kazakhstan	Recommended closing	Require closing	Total border closure
Lao People's Democratic Republic	None to limited measures	None to limited measures	Ban on high-risk region
Malaysia	None to limited measures	None to limited measures	Total border closure
Mongolia	None to limited measures	None to limited measures	Total border closure
Myanmar	Require closing	Require closing	Ban on high-risk region
Nepal	Require closing	Require closing	Total border closure
New Zealand	None to limited measures	None to limited measures	Total border closure
Papua New Guinea	None to limited measures	None to limited measures	Quarantine arrivals
People's Republic of China	Require closing	Require closing	Ban on high-risk region
Philippines	Recommended closing	Recommended closing	Total border closure
Republic of Korea	Recommended closing	None to limited measures	Ban on high-risk region
Singapore	None to limited measures	None to limited measures	Quarantine arrivals
Sri Lanka	None to limited measures	None to limited measures	Total border closure
Thailand	Recommended closing	Recommended closing	Ban on high-risk region
Timor-Leste	None to limited measures	None to limited measures	Ban on high-risk region
Uzbekistan	Require closing	Recommended closing	Total border closure
Vanuatu	None to limited measures	Recommended closing	Total border closure
Viet Nam	Require closing	Recommended closing	Total border closure

ADB = Asian Development Bank, COVID-19 = coronavirus disease.
Note: Some restrictions vary across countries.
Source: University of Oxford. Coronavirus Government Response Tracker (accessed 10 June 2020).

Figure 2: Share of Selected ADB Members with International Transport Restrictions

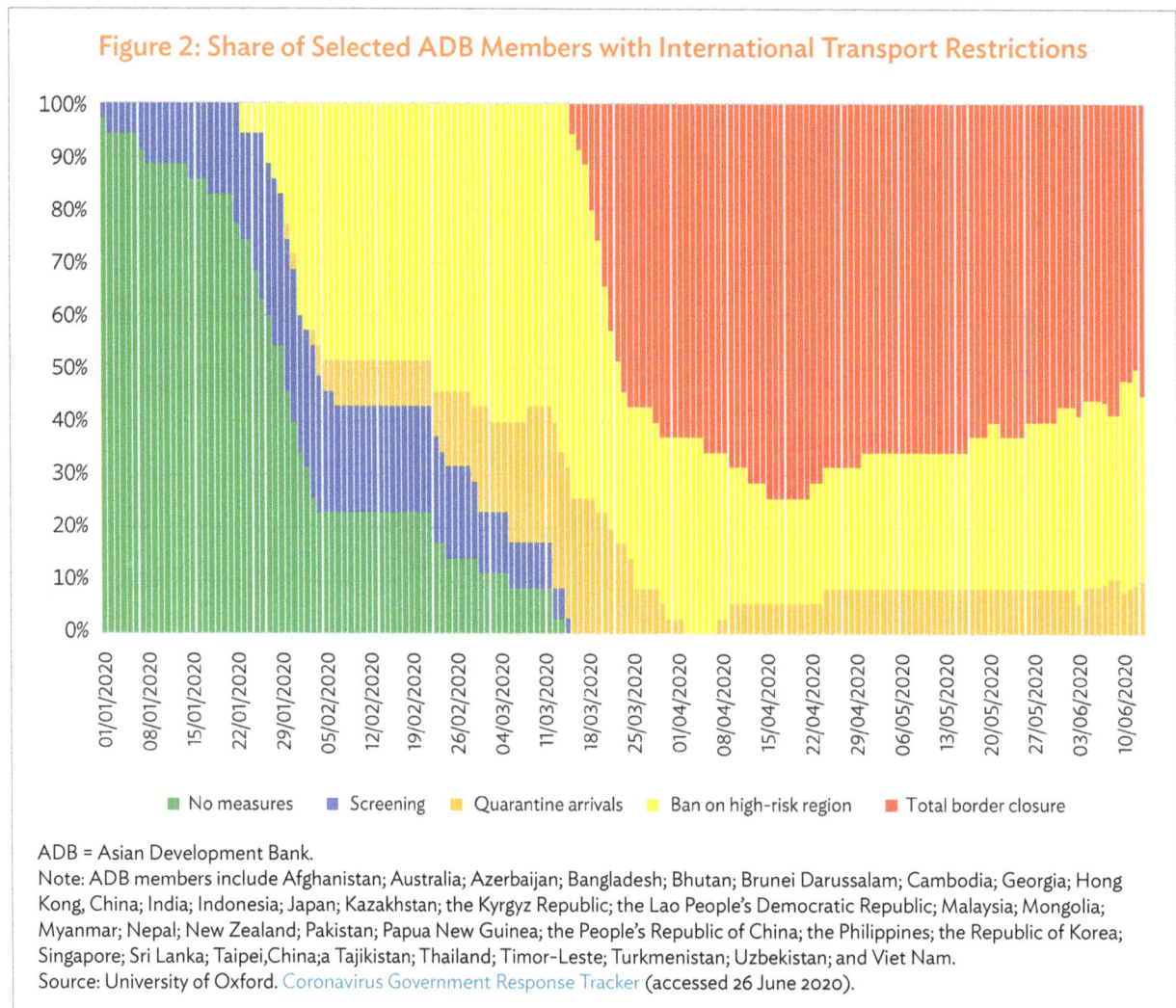

ADB = Asian Development Bank.
Note: ADB members include Afghanistan; Australia; Azerbaijan; Bangladesh; Bhutan; Brunei Darussalam; Cambodia; Georgia; Hong Kong, China; India; Indonesia; Japan; Kazakhstan; the Kyrgyz Republic; the Lao People's Democratic Republic; Malaysia; Mongolia; Myanmar; Nepal; New Zealand; Pakistan; Papua New Guinea; the People's Republic of China; the Philippines; the Republic of Korea; Singapore; Sri Lanka; Taipei,China;a Tajikistan; Thailand; Timor-Leste; Turkmenistan; Uzbekistan; and Viet Nam.
Source: University of Oxford. Coronavirus Government Response Tracker (accessed 26 June 2020).

Continued safe-distancing measures are expected to be part of easing of lockdown, and some organizations have gone as far as advising their employees that they can continue to work from home "forever."[9] While it is likely that remote working will be sustained to differing extents across industries, it is clear that organizations that depend on physical interactions and communication with clients or colleagues may well require employees to return to work at their usual workplace. Split teams and staggered work shifts may be introduced to reduce physical contact and for business contingency purposes. As businesses adapt to the ease of long-distance working facilitated by technology, international business travel could be perceived as less essential in the future.

The potential for working from home is generally believed to be lower in developing Asia than in developed economies. Figure 3 illustrates that, for majority of the developing countries, the share of jobs that can be done from home through telecommuting ranges between 10% and 25%. This is attributed mainly to the economic structure (and therefore types of jobs) and the quality of digital infrastructure in ADB DMCs.[10]

---

9   J. Kelly. 2020. After Announcing Twitter's Permanent Remote-Work Policy, Jack Dorsey Extends Same Courtesy To Square Employees. Forbes. 19 May.
10   International Telecommunication Union data for ADB members indicate that 44% of the population had access to the internet in 2017.

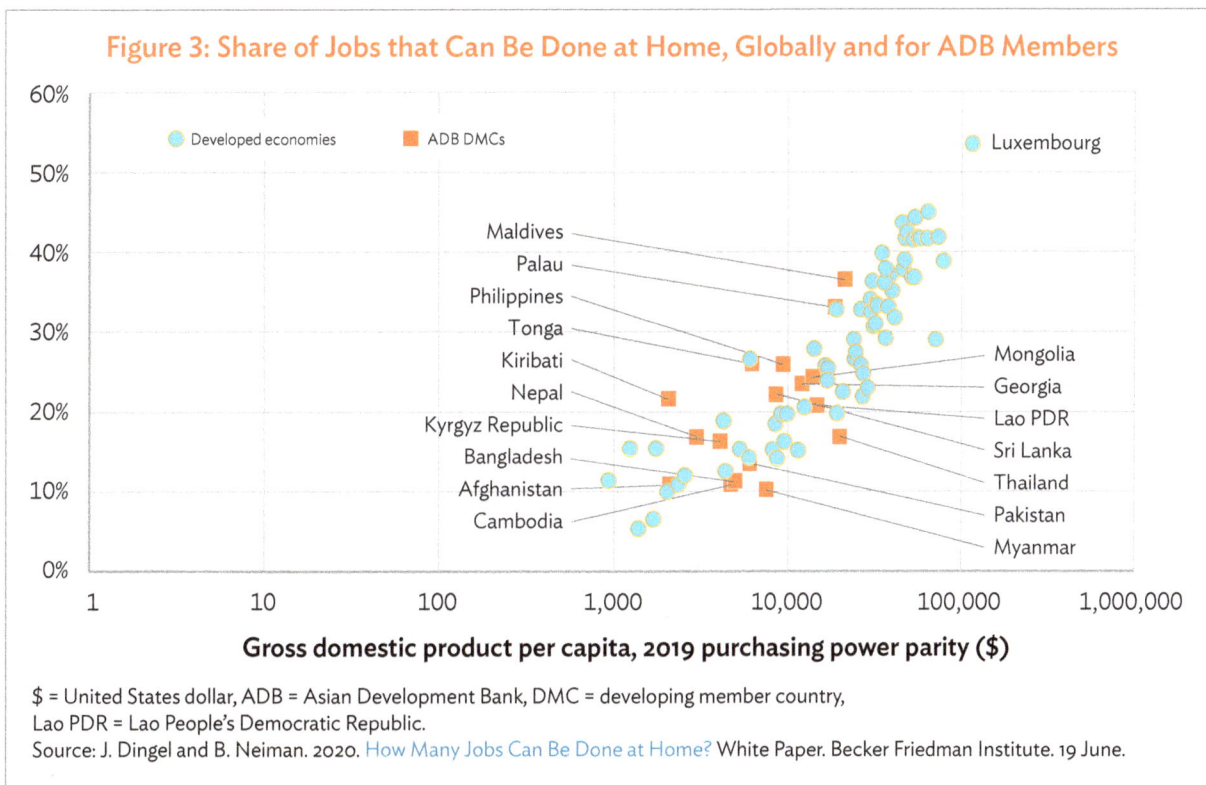

Figure 3: Share of Jobs that Can Be Done at Home, Globally and for ADB Members

$ = United States dollar, ADB = Asian Development Bank, DMC = developing member country,
Lao PDR = Lao People's Democratic Republic.
Source: J. Dingel and B. Neiman. 2020. How Many Jobs Can Be Done at Home? White Paper. Becker Friedman Institute. 19 June.

The behavioral changes above could have a significant impact on trip generation, even after the pandemic. Reduced travel demand and staggered hours will reduce and spread out pre-pandemic peak travel patterns. Working from home could offer substantial travel time savings for employees, which can be used for activities that promote better work–life balance. During the pandemic, this could prove critical in terms of enabling employees to balance their caregiving responsibilities to dependents, such as taking care of the elderly, school-age children, or family members with mobility restrictions.

School

E-learning has been activated on a global scale during this pandemic, forcing a mindset shift among educational leaders, moving away from focusing on attendance days to (online) education hours. Similar to remote working, readily available communication and collaboration tools such as Zoom, Google Meet, and the like have enabled adaptation and transition within this shift. E-learning also implies that physical distance and affordability of travel no longer represent a deterrent.

To minimize disruptions to the school schedule, some countries have managed to keep children at home through a combination of measures including home-based learning and bringing forward school breaks. To adhere to safe-distancing requirements within space constraints, some economies, such as Singapore, have introduced rotating schedules whereby students of different levels take turns to report to school on a weekly basis; home-based learning is conducted on alternate weeks.

For the younger students, keeping them at home could remove walking trips (if the school is close enough), trips on school buses, or drop-offs by private vehicles. For tertiary students, longer distance travel will be eliminated, including local travel and, in the case of international students, international travel. After the pandemic, the e-learning trend is likely to be more sustained for tertiary students than for primary and secondary students. Depending on how long the pandemic lasts, these measures will reduce travel demand in the short term, and the trend could continue in the medium term. Staggered school hours will also minimize congestion on the roads and on public transit.

Online Shopping and Delivery

Widespread safe-distancing measures and lockdowns have resulted in a steep decline in brick-and-mortar shopping. Fueled by fears over food supply disruptions during the pandemic, consumers have flocked to online shopping for panic buying and bulk purchases.[11] For example, online grocery sales in Singapore have increased nearly fourfold since early April.[12] Online food delivery services have also witnessed a surge in demand as consumers continue to take comfort in having familiar foods delivered to them. The surge in e-commerce has created a spike in last-mile delivery, which can cause serious short-term challenges for logistics service providers. However, shifting retail purchases online and consolidating logistics networks in the longer term could contribute to reduced traffic and positive environmental benefits.

Given that human nature governs human interactions, there is no doubt that consumers will return, at least in part, to their old habits once shops reopen. However, as consumers become accustomed to the convenience of online shopping during the pandemic, a dualistic consumption behavior, comprising a mix of offline and online shopping, could be expected to emerge as the new norm.[13] This will have longer-lasting impact on physical trip rates for shopping purposes, which are expected to decrease, balanced with a rise in demand for urban logistics and contactless payment infrastructure.

COVID-19 Travel Demand Impact

The availability of big data from Alphabet Inc.'s Google, Apple Inc., and TomTom through use of maps, apps, and location history provides insights into changes in mobility trends in countries and cities (Box 2).

Figure 4 illustrates aggregated travel behavior across Asia and the Pacific region. National-level data from Apple and Google datasets are combined to develop regional trends. These overall trends indicate a steep decrease in trips across different modes and land use patterns—retail and recreation, essential shopping (groceries and pharmacies), leisure (parks), public transit stations, and workplaces—from March 2020 and into the first half of April 2020. This is matched by a proportionate increase in time spent at places of residence. A similar trend is seen in the relative volume of users' requests for directions for driving, walking, and public transit. A rapid reduction is observed across transit stations and transit use.[14] Toward the end of April to early May 2020, demand gradually recovered across different trip purposes and travel modes. This coincides with an easing of

---

[11] D. Boryso. 2020. E-Commerce Shopping More Frequent because of COVID-19.

[12] S. Choudhury. 2020. Southeast Asia's Online Shopping Boom Is Here to Stay, Even After the Pandemic. *CNBC*. 9 June.

[13] A survey carried out in May 2020 revealed that 85% of respondents would continue purchasing items online even after businesses were open and social distancing measures were lifted. (*Rakuten Insight*. 2020. Online Shopping During and Post Pandemic. 9 June.)

[14] Citymapper. 2020. Mobility Index.

BOX 2

The Use of Big Data to Determine Travel and Mobility Patterns

A key challenge in studying and assessing the impact of the coronavirus disease (COVID-19) on travel demand and activity relates to the availability of up-to-date actual travel activity data. In the absence of reliable travel data, big data offer an opportunity to observe broad trends reflecting the range of government and public responses to COVID-19 around the world. Stakeholders across the world are using such data to enhance contract tracing (with Bluetooth technology), reduce the spread of the virus, and understand mobility behavior and even economic trends. Three major sources of such data are as follows:

(i) Google Mobility dataset. Google collects location data shared by users of Android smartphones and compares the time and duration of visits to locations with the median values on the same day of the week in the 5 weeks from 3 January 2020. The data are broken down by location and display the change in visits to places such as grocery stores and parks. (Google. COVID-19 Community Mobility Reports.)

(ii) Apple Data. This is generated from counting the number of requests made to Apple Maps for directions in selected countries, regions, subregions, and cities. It shows a relative volume of user requests for directions per country, region, subregion, or city compared with a baseline volume on 13 January 2020. (Apple Inc. Mobility Trends Reports.)

(iii) TomTom Traffic Index. This provides a global ranking of urban congestion and compares the current congestion levels with the average congestion in 2019. (TomTom. Traffic Index.)

It is important to note that these are not exhaustive datasets and the sources use different methods to calculate activity. The accuracy may vary significantly from country to country because of user characteristics and smartphone density. Therefore, the data may not represent the travel characteristics of the population as a whole.

Source: Compiled by the Asian Development Bank.

travel restrictions across several Asian countries. Figure 5 shows that, as of 11 June 2020, 19% of ADB members recommended closing of domestic transport and requested people to stay at home, and 35% imposed legal restrictions on domestic transport. About 46% allowed transport with social distancing guidelines. It is important to note that these are regional trends and that substantial differences exist between and, in some cases, within economies.

Figure 4: Change of Share in Mobility Types from Baseline in Selected ADB Members

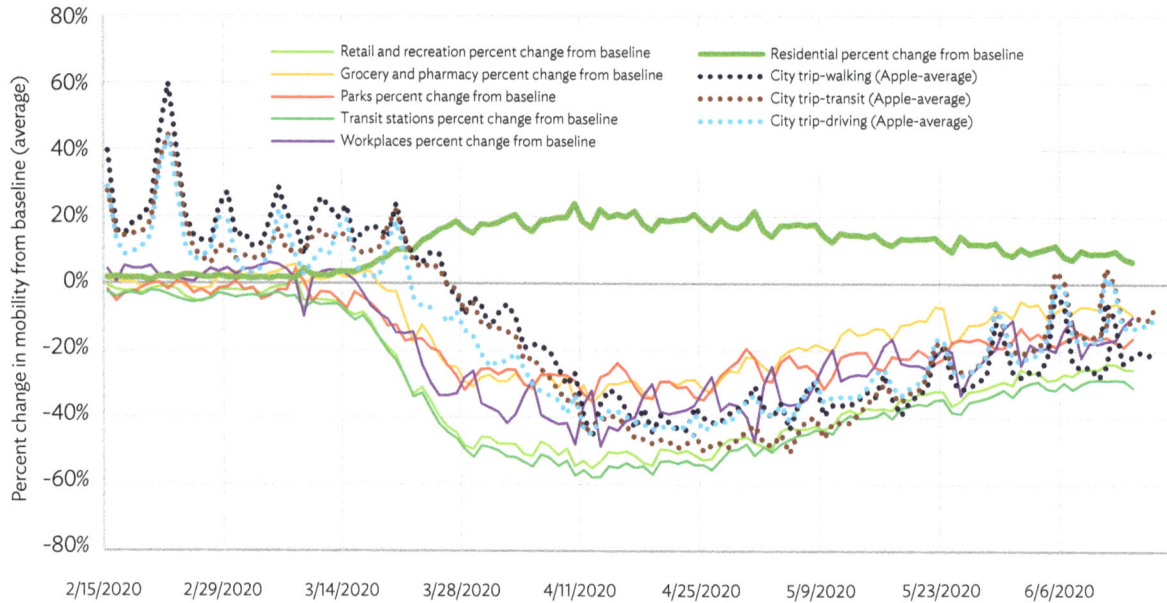

ADB = Asian Development Bank.
Notes:
[1] ADB members include Afghanistan; Australia; Bangladesh; Cambodia; Fiji; Georgia; Hong Kong, China; Indonesia; India; Japan; Kazakhstan; the Kyrgyz Republic; the Lao People's Democratic Republic; Malaysia; Mongolia; Myanmar; Nepal; New Zealand; Pakistan; Papua New Guinea; the Philippines; the Republic of Korea; Singapore; Sri Lanka; Taipei,China; Tajikistan; Thailand; and Viet Nam.
[2] Cities include Adelaide; Auckland; Bangalore; Bangkok; Brisbane; Chandigarh; Changhua; Chennai; Delhi; Denpasar; Fuji; Fukuoka; Hamamatsu; Ha Noi; Hiroshima; Ho Chi Minh City; City of Hong Kong, China; Hsinchu Metropolitan Area; Hyderabad; Islamabad; Jakarta; Kagoshima; Kanazawa; Kitakyushu; Kofu; Kuala Lumpur; Kumamoto; Melbourne; Metro Manila; Mito; Mumbai; Nagoya; Naha; Niigata; Okayama; Osaka; Otsu; Penang; Perth; Phnom Penh; Puducherry; Pune; Sapporo; Sendai; Seoul Capital Area; Singapore; Shizuoka; Sydney; Taoyuan Metropolitan Area; Takamatsu; Takasaki; Tokyo; Toyama; Toyohashi; Tsukuba; Utsunomiya; and Yokkaichi.
Sources: Apple Inc. Mobility Trends Reports (accessed 24 June 2020); and Google. COVID-19 Community Mobility Reports (accessed 24 June 2020).

Figure 5: Share of Selected ADB Members with Restrictions on Domestic Travel

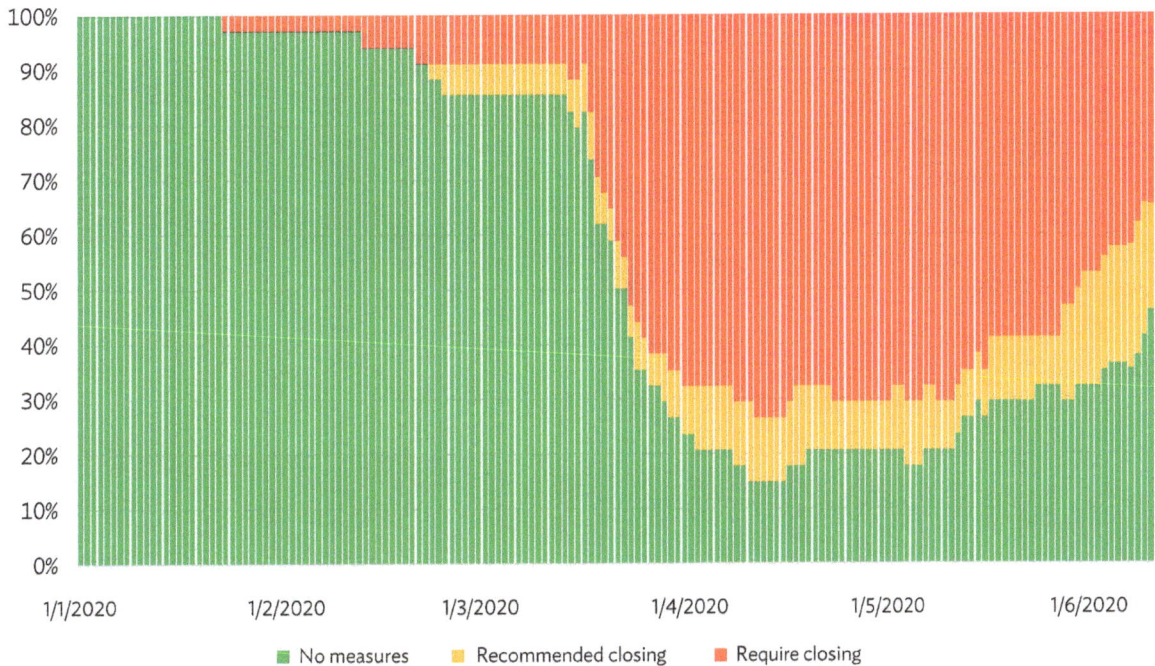

Legend: ■ No measures   ■ Recommended closing   ■ Require closing

ADB = Asian Development Bank.
Note: ADB members include Afghanistan; Australia; Azerbaijan; Bangladesh; Bhutan; Brunei Darussalam; Cambodia; Georgia; Hong Kong, China; India; Indonesia; Japan; Kazakhstan; the Kyrgyz Republic; the Lao People's Democratic Republic; Malaysia; Mongolia; Myanmar; Nepal; New Zealand; Pakistan; Papua New Guinea; the People's Republic of China; the Philippines; the Republic of Korea; Singapore; Sri Lanka; Taipei,China; Tajikistan; Thailand; Timor-Leste; Turkmenistan; Uzbekistan; and Viet Nam.
Source: University of Oxford. Coronavirus Government Response Tracker (accessed 24 June 2020).

Urban Transport

As of 10 June 2020, 26% of ADB members had recommended the closing of urban public transit systems and asked people to stay at home and 19% had a legal requirement to close urban public transit systems. About 56% of economies allowed urban public transit systems to continue operating with social distancing guidelines. The number of restrictions on urban public transit across ADB members peaked between mid-April and mid-May 2020 and has since gradually declined (Figure 6). On 10 June 2020, 19% still required the closure of urban public transit.

Figure 6: Share of Selected ADB Members with Restrictions on Urban Travel

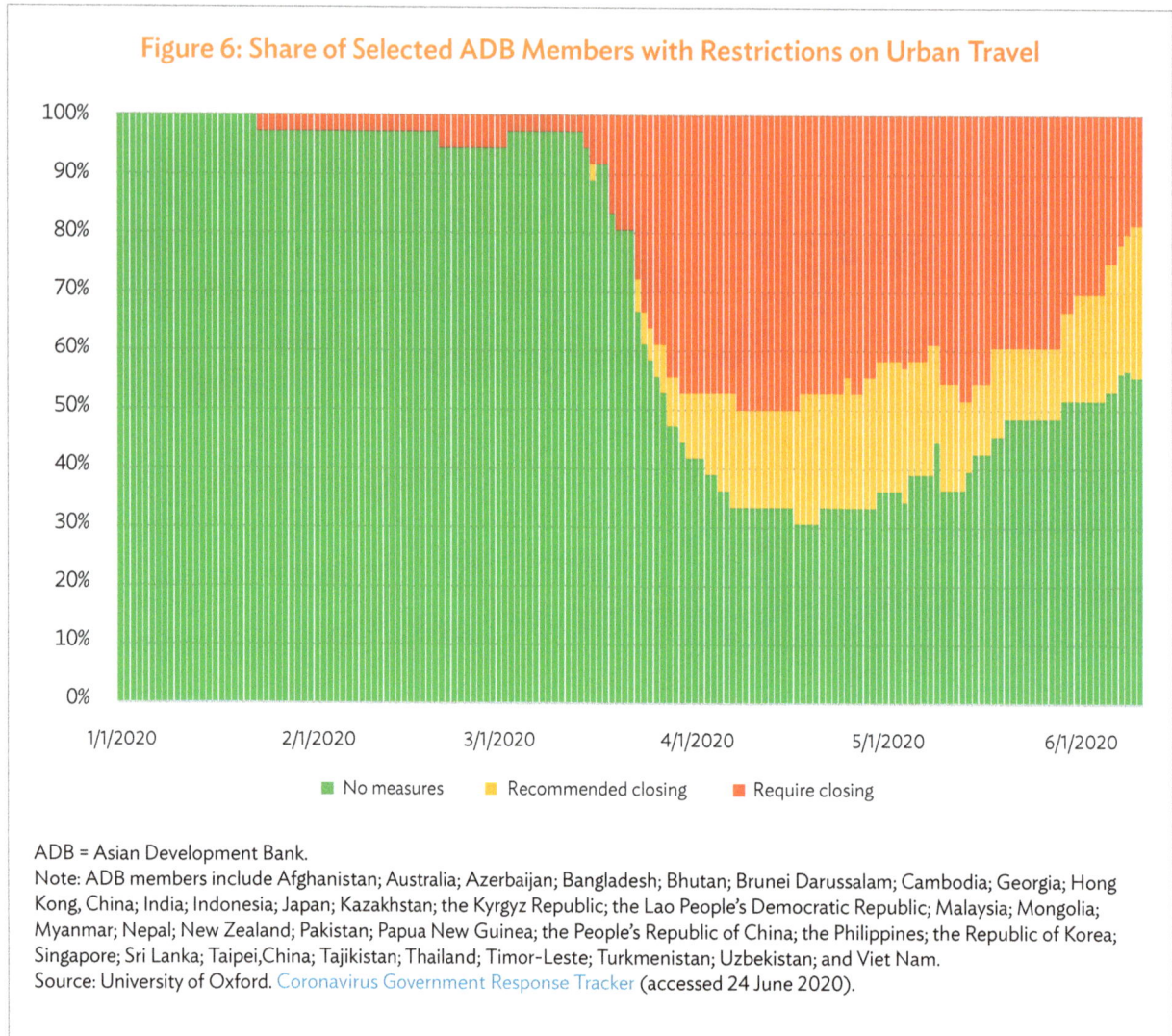

Legend: ■ No measures   ■ Recommended closing   ■ Require closing

ADB = Asian Development Bank.
Note: ADB members include Afghanistan; Australia; Azerbaijan; Bangladesh; Bhutan; Brunei Darussalam; Cambodia; Georgia; Hong Kong, China; India; Indonesia; Japan; Kazakhstan; the Kyrgyz Republic; the Lao People's Democratic Republic; Malaysia; Mongolia; Myanmar; Nepal; New Zealand; Pakistan; Papua New Guinea; the People's Republic of China; the Philippines; the Republic of Korea; Singapore; Sri Lanka; Taipei,China; Tajikistan; Thailand; Timor-Leste; Turkmenistan; Uzbekistan; and Viet Nam.
Source: University of Oxford. Coronavirus Government Response Tracker (accessed 24 June 2020).

Figure 7 shows urban mobility trends derived from Google and Apple big data for 57 cities. The overall trend indicates a steep reduction in urban transport demand across different modes and land use patterns in early April 2020. The highest intensity of reduction is seen for transit use (Appendix 2). Toward the end of April to early May 2020, a gradual recovery of demand was observed across different trip purposes and travel modes. This recovery coincides with the easing of travel restrictions across several Asian cities.

Figure 7: Change of Share in Urban Travel—Public Transit, Walking, and Driving—from Baseline in 50 Asian Cities

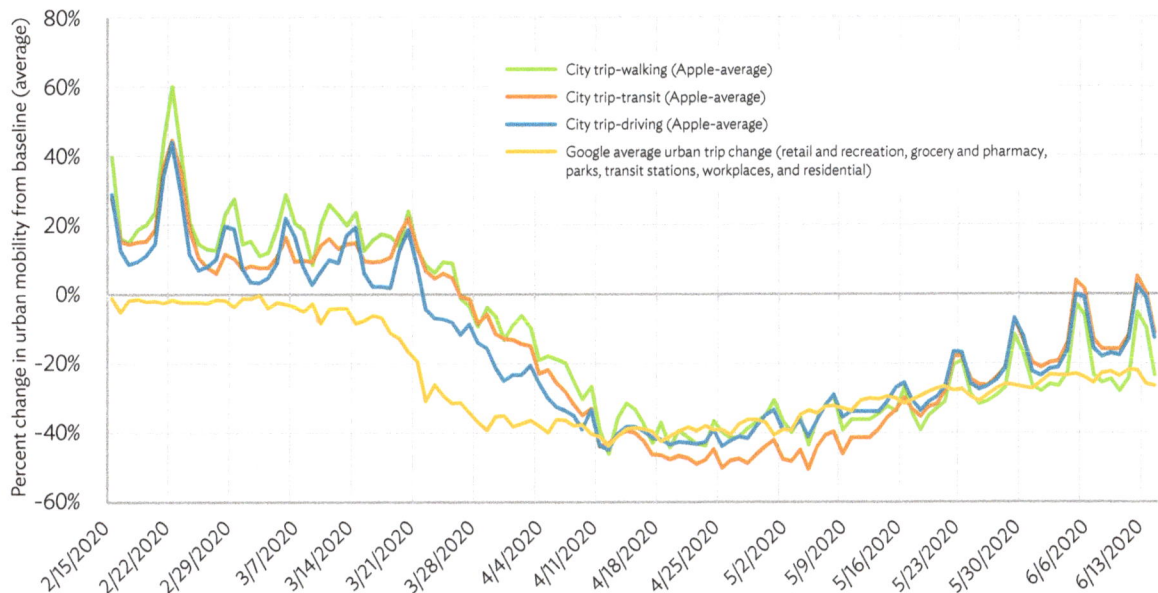

Note: The cities are Adelaide; Auckland; Bangalore; Bangkok; Brisbane; Chandigarh; Changhua Metropolitan Area; Chennai; Delhi; Denpasar; Fuji; Fukuoka; Hamamatsu; Ha Noi; Hiroshima; Ho Chi Minh City; City of Hong Kong, China; Hsinchu Metropolitan Area; Hyderabad; Islamabad; Jakarta; Kagoshima; Kanazawa; Kitakyushu; Kofu; Kuala Lumpur; Kumamoto; Melbourne; Metro Manila; Mito; Mumbai; Nagoya; Naha; Niigata; Okayama; Osaka; Otsu; Penang; Perth; Phnom Penh; Puducherry; Pune; Sapporo; Sendai; Seoul Capital Area; Shizuoka; Singapore; Sydney; Taoyuan Metropolitan Area; Takamatsu; Takasaki; Tokyo; Toyama; Toyohashi; Tsukuba; Utsunomiya; and Yokkaichi.
Sources: Apple Inc. Mobility Trends Reports (accessed 24 June 2020); and Google. COVID-19 Community Mobility Reports (accessed 24 June 2020).

The following trends can be discerned.

Public transit is on the path toward recovery in some cities. On 10 June 2020, public transit ridership was close to the January 2020 baseline trend in Asian cities such as Ha Noi; Ho Chi Minh City; City of Hong Kong, China; Fuji; Hiroshima; Kumamoto; Nagoya; Naha; Niigata; Okayama; Otsu; Sapporo; Sendai; Shizuoka; Takasaki; Toyama; Utsunomiya; and Yokkaichi.

There has been a continued reduction in public transit in others. As of 10 June 2020, visits to transit stations were still significantly reduced relative to the volume of directions requests in January 2020 in Asian cities such as Bali, Delhi, Islamabad, Jakarta, Metro Manila, Melbourne, Mumbai, Phnom Penh, and Singapore.

Demand for driving and walking is increasing. The demand for driving and walking is increasing more rapidly than demand for public transit but with some exceptions, where these modes remain well below pre-COVID-19 levels.[15]

---

[15] In the case of Beijing, bike sharing levels went up by 187% in April. (D. Liu, L. Xue, and T. Huang. 2020. 3 Ways China's Transport Sector Is Working to Recover from Covid-19 Lockdowns. *The City Fix*. 30 April.)

Further disaggregated trends on driving, transit, and walking have been observed in individual economies depending on the differing extent of restrictions on movements imposed as well as access to private modes of transport. Further details are provided in Appendix 3.

Restrictions on driving (personal cars) have led to temporary reductions in congestion in affected cities. Figure 8 shows how lockdown tended to result in a sharp drop in congestion levels followed by a gradual increase in 18 Asian cities. The congestion data follow the urban mobility trends described. Congestion levels have not yet returned to the levels seen before the COVID-19 outbreak but, as the economy starts to recover, this is likely to be the case.

One lesson that can be drawn from observed data is that a rapid resurgence of traffic could occur once movement restrictions are lifted. This leaves a very brief window of opportunity for cities to implement measures to promote the uptake of low-carbon alternatives to lock in the improved air quality gains achieved during the peak of global travel and movement restrictions.

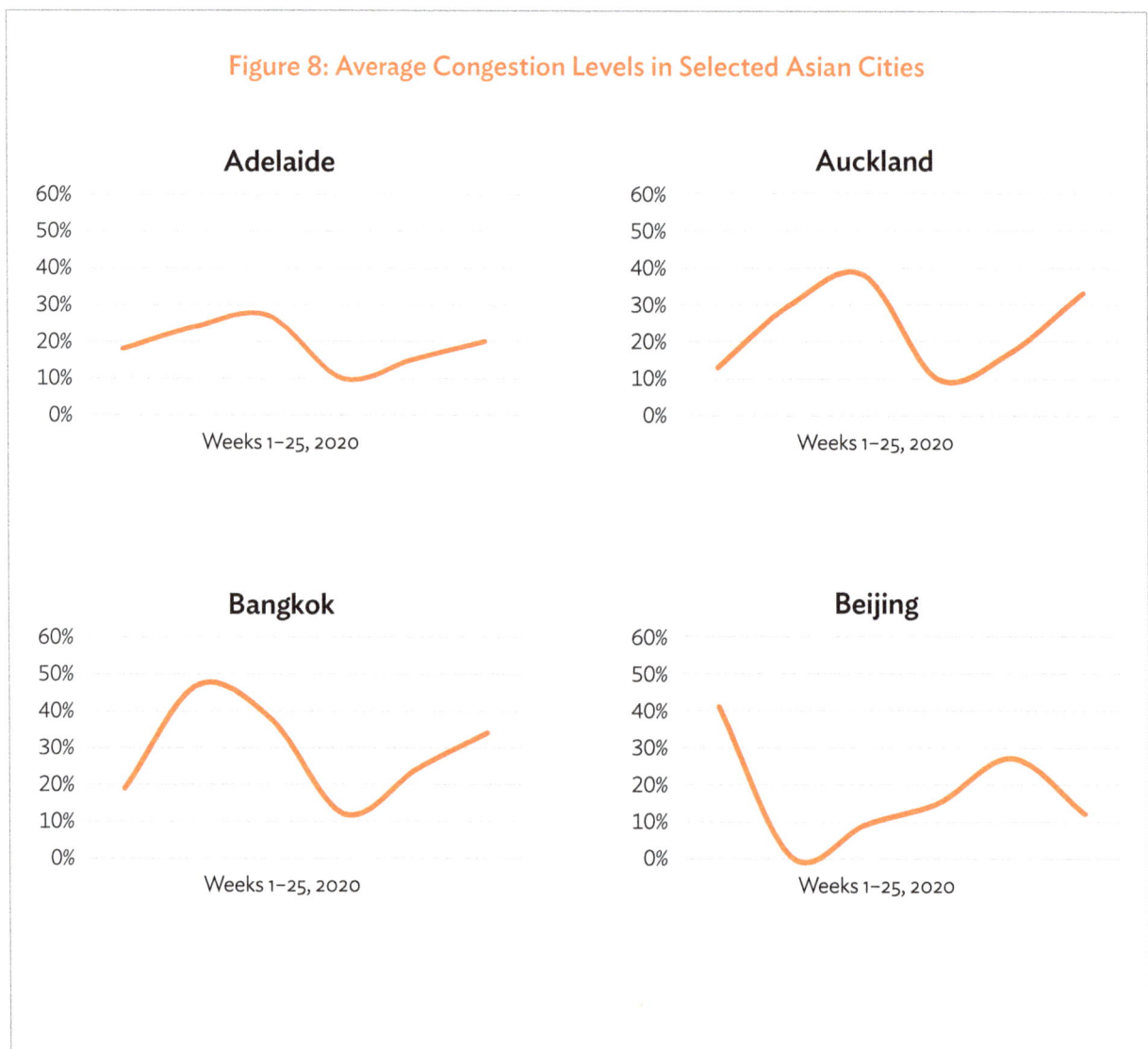

Figure 8: Average Congestion Levels in Selected Asian Cities

Figure 8 *continued*

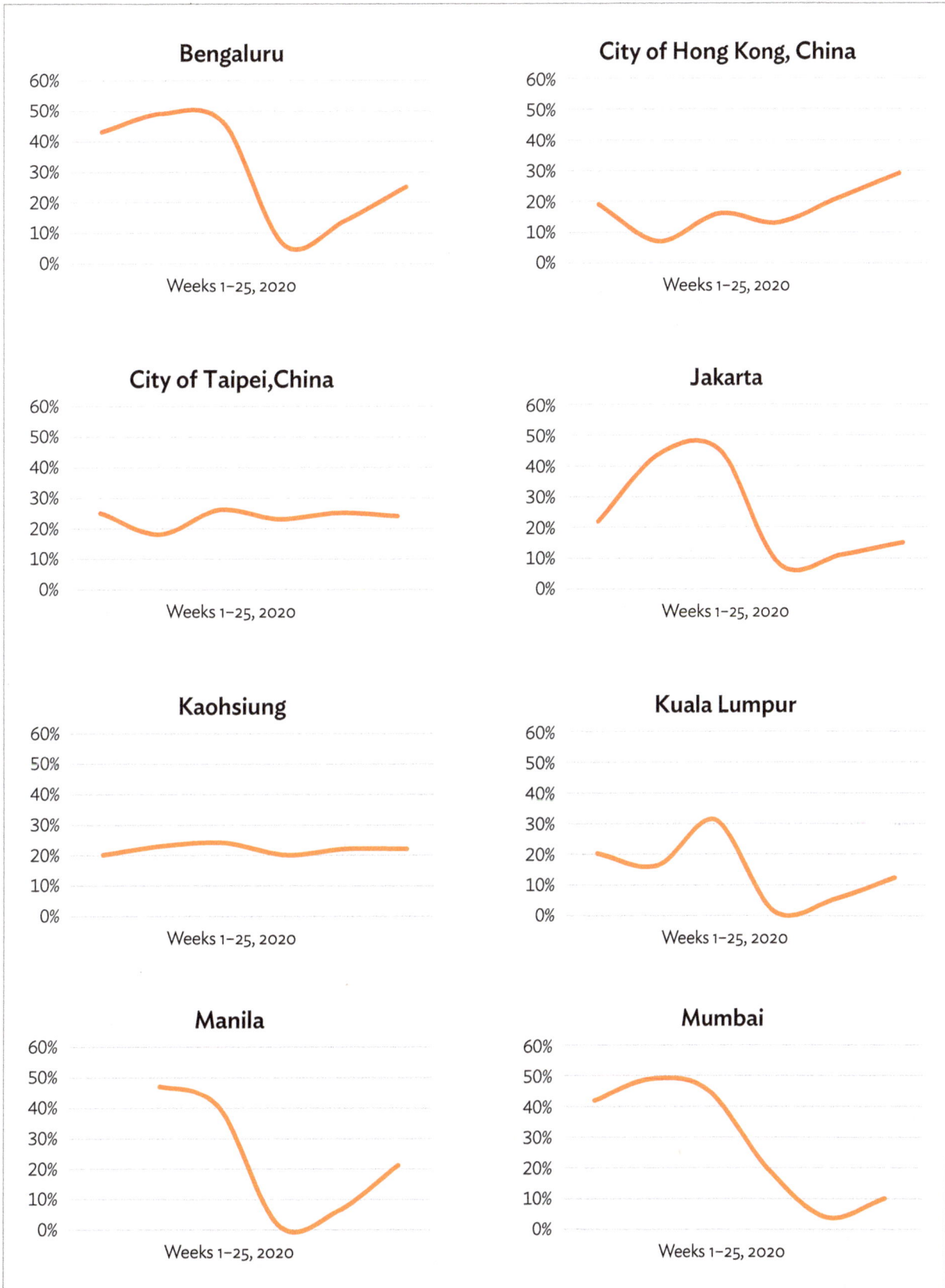

Bengaluru

Weeks 1–25, 2020

City of Hong Kong, China

Weeks 1–25, 2020

City of Taipei,China

Weeks 1–25, 2020

Jakarta

Weeks 1–25, 2020

Kaohsiung

Weeks 1–25, 2020

Kuala Lumpur

Weeks 1–25, 2020

Manila

Weeks 1–25, 2020

Mumbai

Weeks 1–25, 2020

continued on next page

Figure 8 *continued*

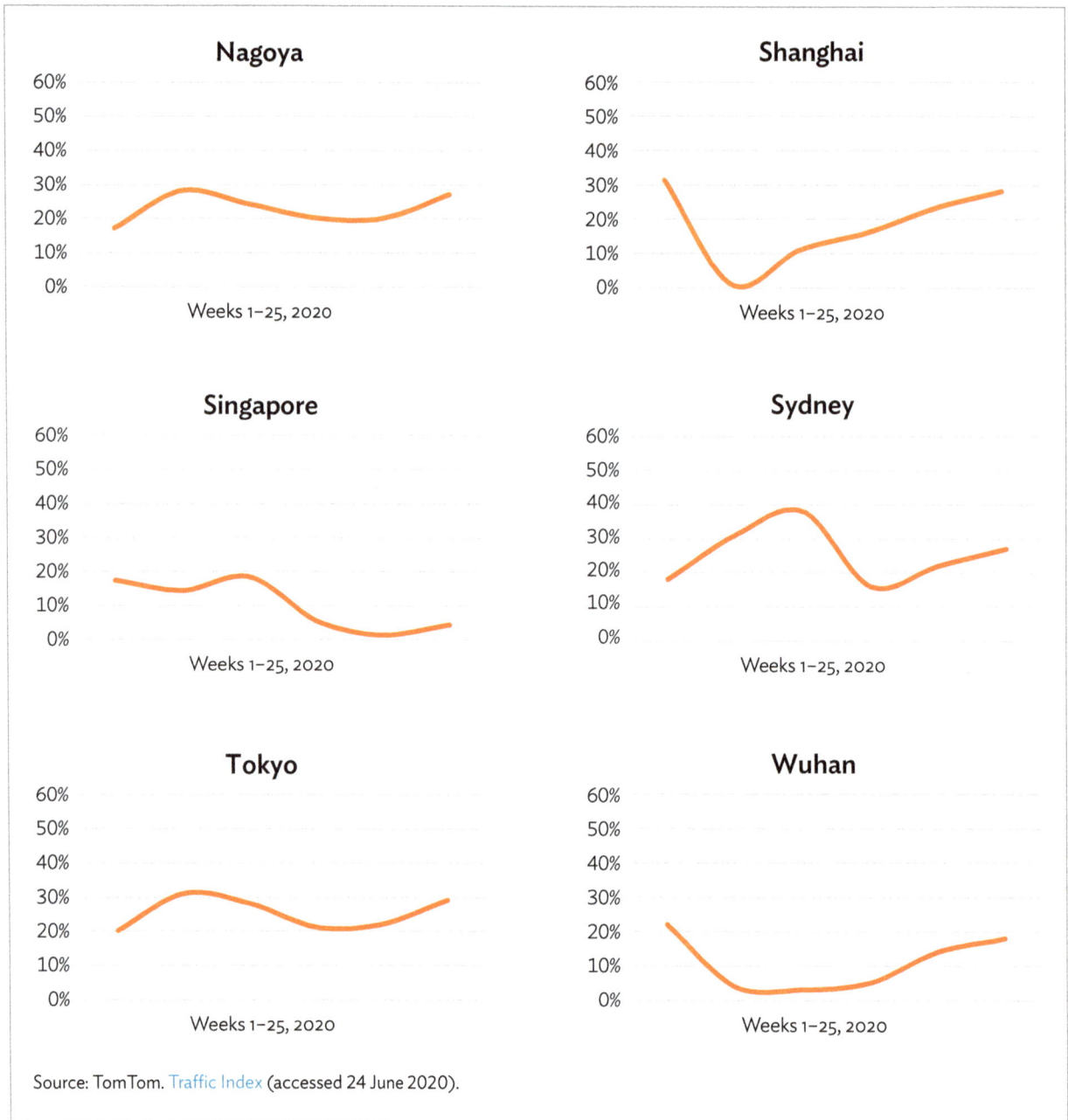

Source: TomTom. Traffic Index (accessed 24 June 2020).

Private Transport—Car Sales

In parallel with the decline in private driving in most Asian cities during the lockdown phase, automotive sales have collapsed in many of the major vehicle markets in Asia (Table 2). Where restrictions have been lifted, sales are returning, in some cases toward earlier levels.

In the gradual recovery of automotive sales, a consumer preference for electric vehicles over traditional gasoline and diesel vehicles has been observed in some markets.[16]

---

[16] K. Stock. 2020. As COVID-19 Hits Electric Vehicles, Some Thrive, Others Die. *Bloomberg.* 19 May.

Table 2: Automotive and Motorcycle Sales during COVID-19

Country	Automotive and Motorcycle Sales
India[a]	In May, India's top passenger vehicle manufacturer, Maruti Suzuki, reported sales about 89% lower than in the same month in 2019. Overall, compared with May 2019, total sales were down by nearly 85%.
Indonesia[b]	Indonesia's vehicle production slumped by 80.8% on the month to 21,434 units in April, and 79.5% lower from 104,622 units in 2019. April 2020's light-duty vehicle sales reduced by more than 90% year-on-year to 7,871 units.
Japan[c]	In May 2020, automobile sales dropped nearly 55% year-on-year to 218,285 vehicles, compared with a 29% year-on-year decline in April.
Malaysia[d]	Automobile sales in Malaysia reduced by 62% to 22,960 units in May 2020 from 60,760 units in May 2019.
People's Republic of China[c]	In April 2020, passenger vehicle sales were almost back to pre-COVID-19 levels of growth, with sales up 4.4% year-on-year to 2.1 million units. May 2020 saw further improvement, with sales rising 12% year-on-year to 2.1 million vehicles.
Philippines[e]	Light-duty vehicle sales reduced by 65% in March 2020.
Republic of Korea[f]	Vehicle sales in May 2020 reduced by 36% compared with May 2019 sales.
Thailand[g]	Light-duty vehicle sales reduced by about 65% in April 2020 and 54% in May 2020, compared with 2019 sales for April and May. Motorcycles sales reduced by 39% in May 2020, compared with May 2019.
Viet Nam[h]	Light-duty vehicle sales are reported at 64,100 units in the first 4 months of 2020, down 36% year-on-year. Motorcycles sales fell by 71% in April 2020.

COVID-19 = coronavirus disease.
[a] FE Bureau. 2020. Covid-19 Lockdown: Vehicle Sales Pick Up in May as Production, Dealerships Restart. *Express Drives*. 2 June.
[b] C. Choo and S. Chin. 2020. ASEAN Carmakers Face Bleak 2020 as Coronavirus Pandemic Cripples Demand. *S&P Global Platts*. 28 May; and M. Parama. 2020. Automakers Slash Car Sales Targets as Spending Power Weakens. *The Jakarta Post*. 20 May.
[c] V. Piparsania. 2020. Weekly Update: COVID-19 Impact on Global Automotive Industry. *Counterpoint*. 14 July.
[d] *Malay Mail*. 2020. Vehicle Sales in Malaysia 62pc Lower in May, say MAA. 22 June.
[e] A. L. E. Gonzales. 2020. March Auto Sales down 65% on COVID Impact. *The Manila Times*. 6 June.
[f] Yonhap. 2020. Auto Sales Dip 36% in May amid Pandemic. *The Korea Herald*. 1 June.
[g] *Reuters*. 2020. Thai May Domestic Car Sales Tumble 54.12% y/y – Industries Federation. 18 June.
[h] N. Thuy. 2020. Vietnam Takes New Tax Step to Stimulate Car Market. *Hanoi Times*. 29 May; and MotorCycles Data. 2020. Vietnam: Motorcycles Sales Fell Down 71% in April. 27 May.
Source: Compiled by the Asian Development Bank.

Air Travel

The International Air Transport Association (IATA) reports drastic demand decreases across several global indicators. In March 2020, global passenger traffic, measured in total revenue passenger kilometers (RPKs), was 52.9% lower than in March 2019; capacity (available seat kilometers) was 36.2% lower; and the load factor was 21.4% lower.[17] Given that the PRC was the first epicenter of the pandemic, airlines in Asia and the Pacific were initially more severely affected than the other global airlines. In early April 2020, there were 80% fewer flights globally than in April 2019.[18] Most signs point toward a slow recovery in the coming months and possibly years.

---

[17] IATA. 2020. Passenger Demand Plunges in March as Travel Restrictions Take Hold. **Press Release No. 36. 29 April.**
[18] IATA. 2020. COVID-19 Puts Over Half of 2020 Passenger Revenues at Risk. **Press Release No. 29. 14 April.**

The IATA expects overall passenger volumes to fall by about 50% in 2020.[19] The recovery of passenger volumes will depend on a range of factors including progress and timing of containment of the virus in countries, reopening of international borders, availability of a vaccine, and restored consumer confidence. Even when the strict bans on entry and visa applications are removed, quarantine requirements are likely to discourage passengers from making leisure or business trips in the short term.

Forecasts by the IATA in April 2020 estimated the global RPKs for 2021 to be 32%–41% lower than pre-COVID-19 levels (Figure 9). Estimates from the International Civil Aviation Organization in June 2020 indicate that the economic loss in Asia and the Pacific alone could be in the range of $100 billion–$130 billion.[20] However, it is expected that global aviation will continue to improve gradually up to 2025, with a global RPK estimate of 10% lower than pre-COVID-19 level.

Freight and Logistics

The COVID-19 outbreak has also significantly affected the logistics sector through disruptions in services, as employees of manufacturing, logistics, and customs operations were affected by the lockdowns and reduced economic activity. The International Transport Forum estimates that mobility restrictions to contain COVID-19 could reduce global freight transport demand by up to 36% by the end of 2020.[21]

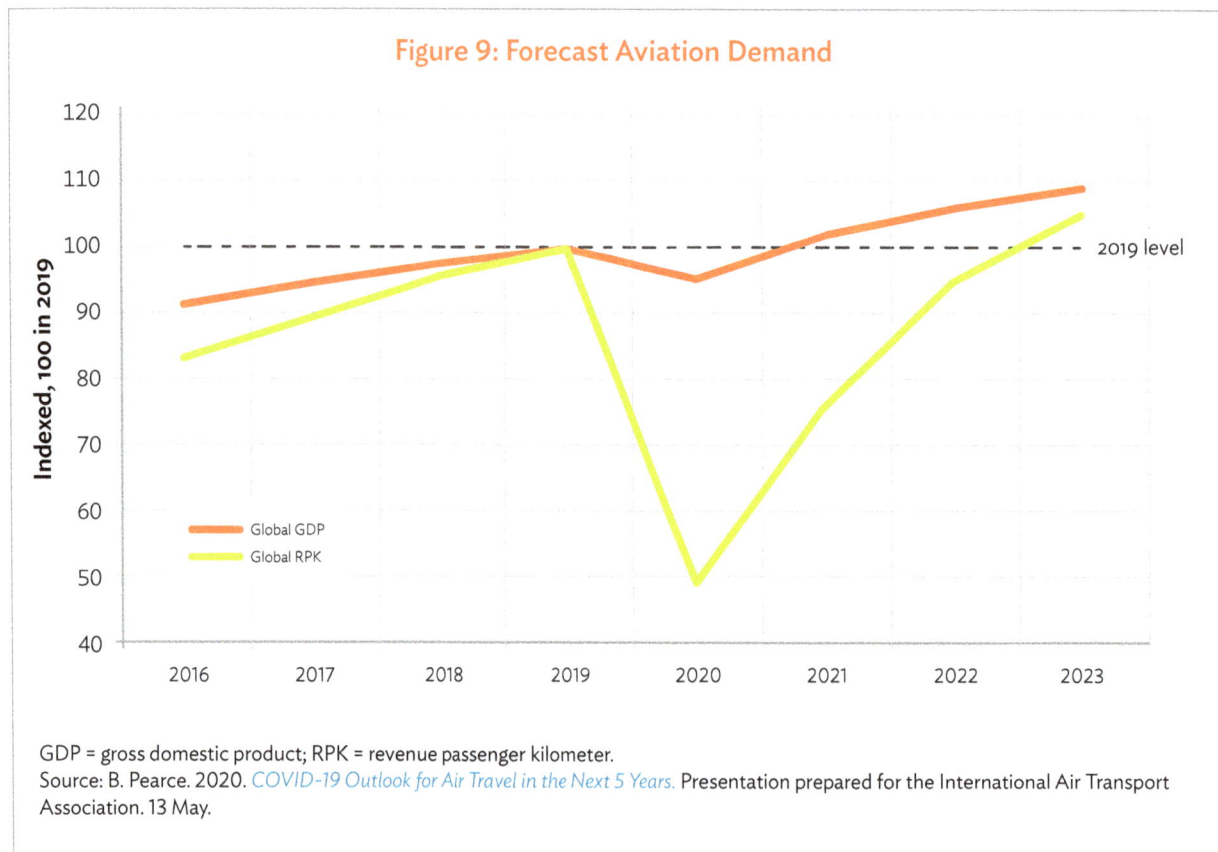

Figure 9: Forecast Aviation Demand

GDP = gross domestic product; RPK = revenue passenger kilometer.
Source: B. Pearce. 2020. *COVID-19 Outlook for Air Travel in the Next 5 Years.* Presentation prepared for the International Air Transport Association. 13 May.

[19] IATA. 2020. Recovery in Air Travel Expected to Lag Economic Activity. IATA Economics' Chart of the Week. 15 May.
[20] Air Transport Bureau. 2020. Effects of Novel Coronavirus (COVID-19) on Civil Aviation: Economic Impact Analysis. Presentation prepared for the International Civil Aviation Organization. Montreal, Canada. 24 November.
[21] International Transport Forum. 2020. How Badly will the Coronavirus Crisis Hit Global Freight? COVID-19 Transport Brief. 11 May.

Air cargo has been the most severely disrupted mode. Airlines transported more than 52 million tons of goods in 2019, representing more than 35% of global trade by value but less than 1% by volume. Although this is a small percentage, air freight has played an essential role in transporting high-value commodities. Typically, dedicated freighters carry less than half of global air freight demand (in terms of freight-tonne-kilometers). Hence, the loss of the belly cargo capacity of scheduled passenger flights has led to a large cargo capacity shortfall, resulting in a surge in air cargo rates. Figure 10 indicates that, compared with March 2019, March 2020 saw a reduction in global air freight capacity by about 25%, largely because of the cancelation of passenger flights that also carry cargo, but also because of a 15% reduction in air freight demand (in cargo tonne-kilometers) in response to the economic downturn caused by COVID-19. Asia and the Pacific saw the second-largest regional decline after the Latin America region.

About 80% of the world's trade is carried by sea. As the world's factory, the PRC is home to 7 of the world's 10 busiest container ports. The COVID-19 outbreak has led to a significant decrease in the number of ships calling. In Shanghai, the largest port in the world, and Yangshang, the number of port calls had declined by 17% in January 2020 compared with the same period in the previous year. This created a knock-on effect globally, with several ports seeing cargo volumes decline. The port of Los Angeles, the largest container port in the US, announced a year-on-year fall in cargo volumes of about 25% in February 2020. As the virus continues to spread, together with

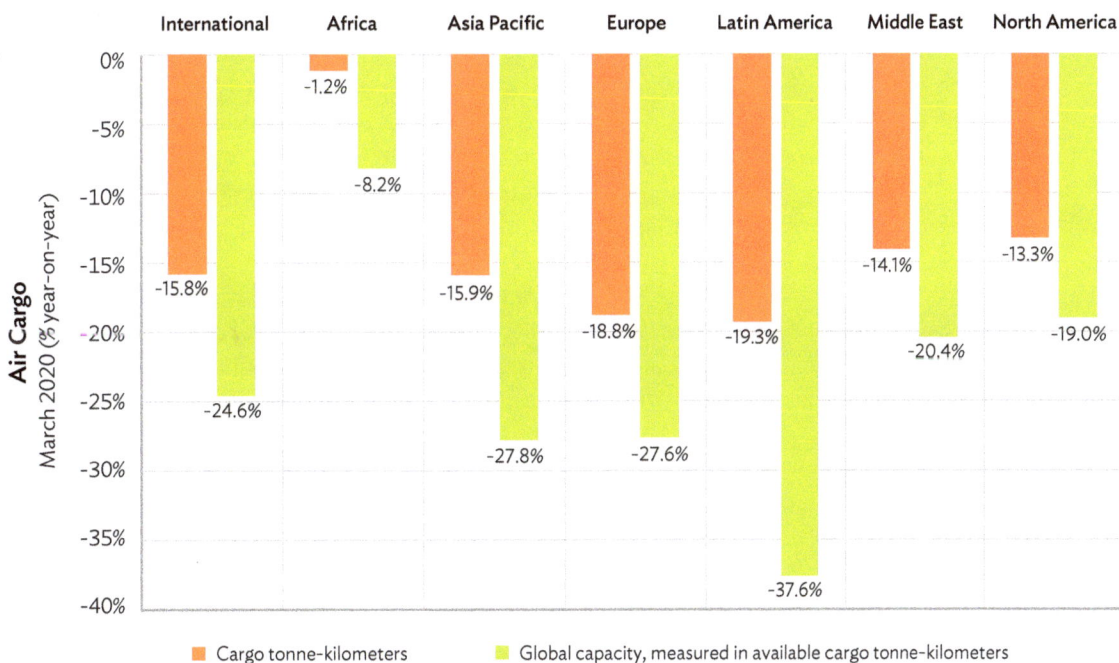

Figure 10: Air Cargo Activity and Capacity in March 2020, Compared with March 2019

Source: International Air Transport Association. 2020. Passenger Demand Plunges in March as Travel Restrictions Take Hold. Press Release No. 36. 29 April.

the ongoing US trade war, global shipping demand is expected to decline further.[22] Shipping data, based on real-time observations of vessel positions, showed a 17%–18% reduction in container ship unique weekly port visits in Asia during February and March 2020.[23]

The impact on rail freight movement has been mixed. In the PRC, China National Railway statistics reveal that railway freight carried between the PRC and Europe during Q1 2020 had increased by 24% compared with the same period in 2019.[24] However, in India, rail freight traffic in April and May 2020 had decreased by 28% compared with 2019 demand.[25]

Transport Needs of Different User Groups, Including Vulnerable Groups

Even in restrictive lockdown conditions, essential services must be maintained to ensure continuity of necessary goods and services to sustain life. Although the list of essential services varies across the different countries, it typically comprises sectors relating to health and social services, food supply, importers and exporters, logistics and distribution, aviation, shipping, public transit, banking and finance, and law and order. It may also include other sectors such as water and sanitation, which are vital to avoid exacerbating transmission. In developed countries, such as Japan and Singapore, it is estimated that the minimum essential workforce could be about 15%–20% of the total workforce in times of pandemic.[26]

In developing Asia, commuters rely mainly on informal public transit modes or "paratransit" services such as jeepneys, minivans, and shared vehicles. Like businesses everywhere, the COVID-19 restrictions have hit these modes of transport services severely. Governments have enforced a complete ban or legislated social distancing amid rising cases of COVID-19. The operators of informal paratransit are at greater risk because of their small operating profits, limited financial literacy, lack of access to finance, and fragmented ownership structures.[27]

During the pandemic, the elderly proved to be more vulnerable to COVID-19. As they have been advised to stay home, they require social care and access to food, basic supplies, money, and medicine to support their physical health.[28] In the PRC, residents, government staff, and voluntary groups came together during the lockdown to provide support by delivering food and necessities to designated areas to minimize human-to-human contact.[29]

[22] *Ship Technology*. 2020. COVID-19 Outbreak could Force Shipping Industry into Yet Another Crisis. 23 March.

[23] A. Zein. 2020. Short-Term Effects of the Coronavirus Outbreak: What Does the Shipping Data Say? United Nations Conference on Trade and Development Transport and Trade Facilitation Newsletter. Article No. 48. 4 March; and *Hellenic Shipping News*. 2020. Overview of COVID-19 and Its Impact on Shipping Behaviour. 16 June.

[24] *Logistics Bureau*. 2020. 2020 Trends in Freight Transportation, and the COVID-19 Impact. 16 June.

[25] S. Jacob and S. Jai. 2020. Rail Freight Traffic Drops 28% in April–May amid COVID-19 Lockdown. *Business Standard*. 7 June.

[26] T. F. Tay. 2020. Coronavirus: Last Digit of IC to Determine Entry to Four Markets; Essential Workforce to Be Cut to 15 Per Cent. *The Straits Times*. 21 April; and T. Mochizuki, L. Du, and G. Allan. 2020. Japan Emergency Decree Shuts Headquarters, Nintendo Flagship. *Bloomberg*. 7 April.

[27] A. D. San Juan. 2020. Traditional Jeepney Operators Unsure when LTFRB Will Allow them To Resume Operation. *Manila Bulletin*. 25 June.

[28] H. H. Kluge. 2020. Supporting Older People during the COVID-19 Pandemic Is Everyone's Business. World Health Organization Regional Office for Europe. 3 April.

[29] B. Li and B. Lu. 2020. How China Made Its COVID-19 Lockdown Work. *East Asia Forum*. 7 April.

For low-income groups, working from home is often not a viable option, particularly for those in service-related jobs such as in homes, restaurants, retail, farming, and manufacturing. Staying at home would mean losing their livelihood and income. This makes it difficult for this group to take precautionary measures during a pandemic. Any disruption in the food supply chain or inflationary prices would affect this group most, possibly resulting in hunger. To exacerbate their problems, they are least likely to have access to health care. Low-income groups in developing countries also have the lowest rates of access to internet, making it hard for them to work from home or participate in online learning.

For many underprivileged children, stay-at-home policies not only have impact on learning but also create a greater risk of hunger, as school meals typically constitute the most nutritious meal of the day for such children.[30] In such cases, local governments could make appropriate provisions for vulnerable children to continue to travel to schools. Provided schools put in place precautionary measures, this could be a safer option for these children.

Travel demand will be substantially reduced for vulnerable groups during a lockdown. Transport plays an important role in keeping core infrastructure open to ensure necessities, health-care services, and aid reach vulnerable groups. Advanced technology could a be harnessed to monitor and coordinate responses to ensure the needs of these groups are met. In the post-recovery period, travel demand for the vulnerable groups, particularly the low-income and underprivileged children, is expected to rebound to pre-COVID-19 unless policy restrictions are put in place.

Impact on the Environment, Road Safety, and Economy

Climate Change and Air Pollution

Before COVID-19, transport contributed to about 24% of carbon emissions directly related to global energy.[31] The lockdowns put in place had a direct impact on CO_2 emissions from transport both globally and in rapidly growing Asian economies (Figure 11). The transport sector is estimated to have made the largest contribution to COVID-19-related CO_2 emission reductions. The initial impact in the transport sector (in early March 2020) was in Asia and the Pacific region, with other regions contributing significantly in April and May 2020. As lockdowns are relaxed and transport demand increases again, transport-related CO_2 emissions are expected to rebound.[32]

---

[30] United Nations World Food Programme. School Feeding.
[31] International Energy Agency. 2020. *Tracking Transport 2020*. Paris.
[32] C. Le Quere et al. 2020. Temporary Reduction in Daily Global CO2 Emissions during the COVID-19 Forced Confinement. *Nature Climate Change*. 10. pp. 647–653.

Figure 11: Transport-Related Carbon Dioxide Emissions of Selected Asian Economies and Globally
(million tons daily reduction)

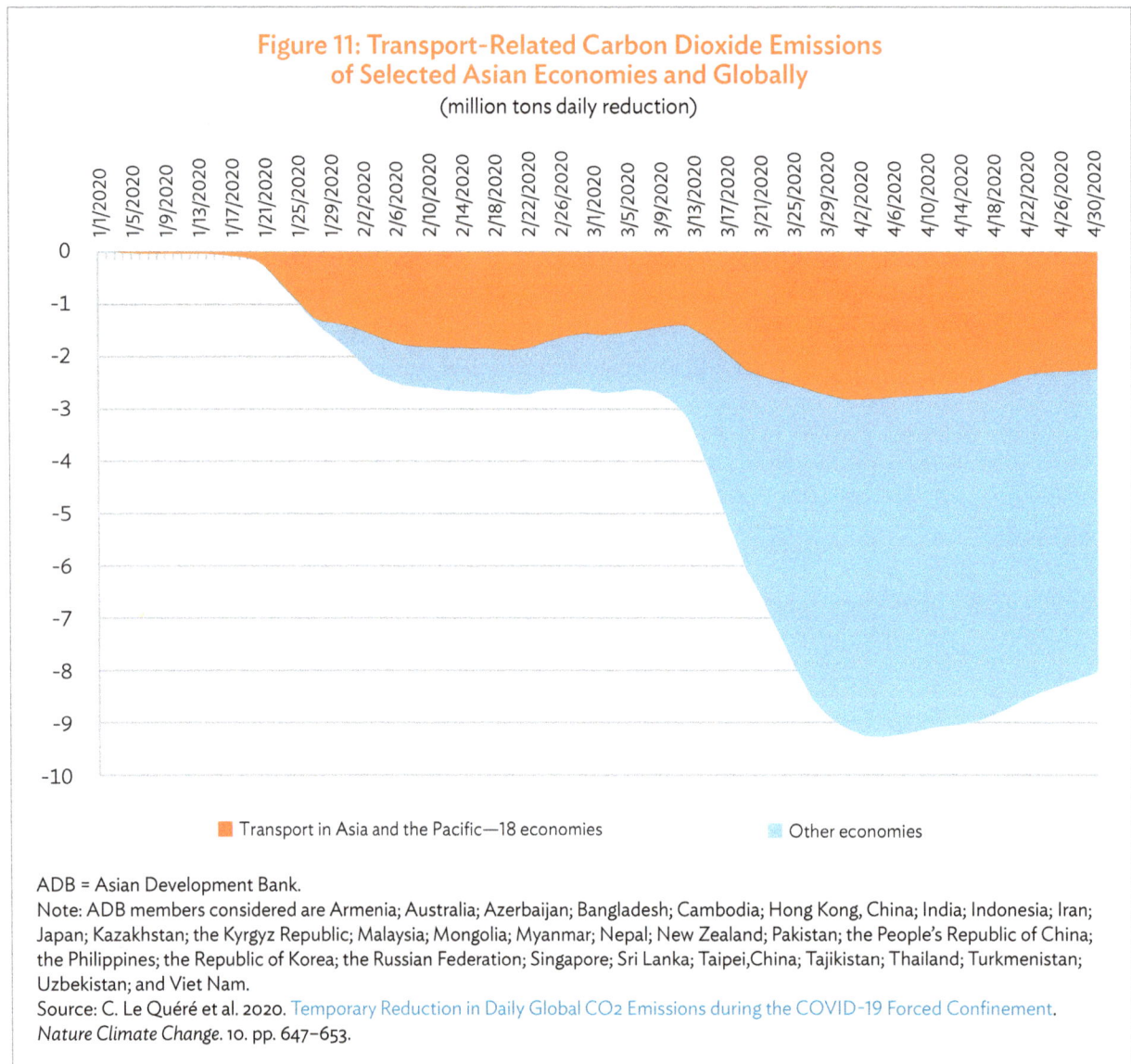

■ Transport in Asia and the Pacific—18 economies   ■ Other economies

ADB = Asian Development Bank.
Note: ADB members considered are Armenia; Australia; Azerbaijan; Bangladesh; Cambodia; Hong Kong, China; India; Indonesia; Iran; Japan; Kazakhstan; the Kyrgyz Republic; Malaysia; Mongolia; Myanmar; Nepal; New Zealand; Pakistan; the People's Republic of China; the Philippines; the Republic of Korea; the Russian Federation; Singapore; Sri Lanka; Taipei,China; Tajikistan; Thailand; Turkmenistan; Uzbekistan; and Viet Nam.
Source: C. Le Quéré et al. 2020. Temporary Reduction in Daily Global CO2 Emissions during the COVID-19 Forced Confinement. *Nature Climate Change*. 10. pp. 647–653.

Depending on the magnitude and intensity of restrictive measures for transport, total CO_2 emissions related to domestic transport in Asian countries could be 21%–26% lower in 2020 than they were in 2019 (Figure 12). Forecasting beyond 2020 is difficult as much depends on how the economy develops after the restrictions are lifted.

In Wuhan, where lockdown was first introduced, nitrogen dioxide (NO_2) levels were observed to have halved in February 2020 compared with average February levels in 2014–2019.[33] Figure 13 shows satellite images of NO_2 emissions over the PRC. The levels of particulate matter less than 2.5 micrometers in diameter ($PM_{2.5}$) fell by about a quarter in the same period. Emissions increased in March 2020 as road traffic and industrial activity began to resume.[34]

---

[33] NO2 is a major pollutant that is closely linked to road traffic emissions and industrial activity. It can therefore be a good indicator of economic activity.
[34] M. Henriques. 2020. Will COVID-19 Have a Lasting Impact on the Environment? *BBC*. 27 March.

Figure 12: Domestic Transport Emissions of ADB Members in 2020

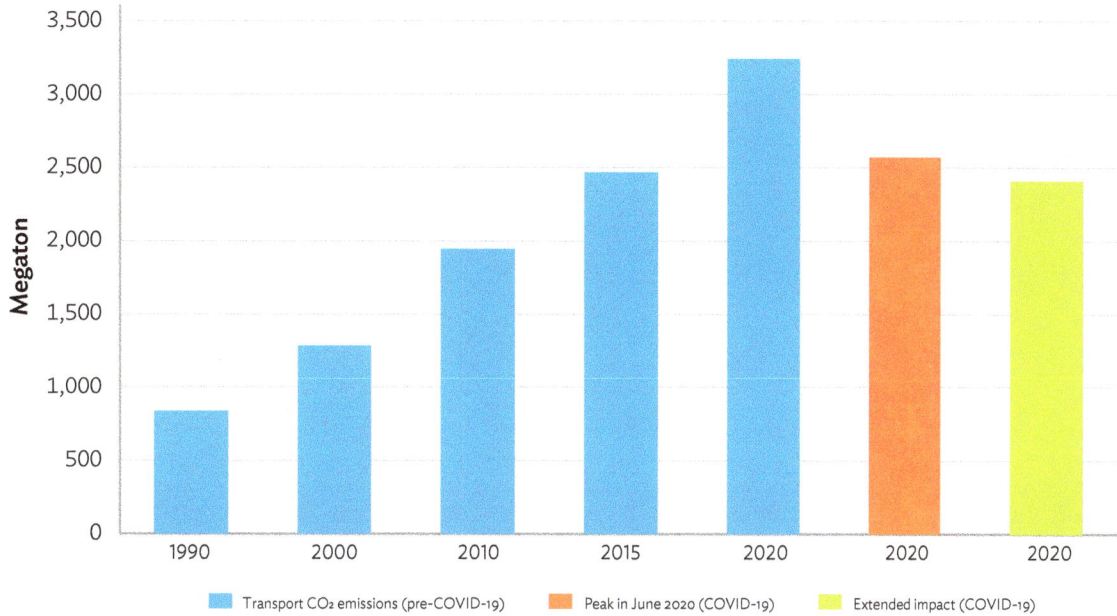

Legend:
- Transport CO_2 emissions (pre-COVID-19)
- Peak in June 2020 (COVID-19)
- Extended impact (COVID-19)

ADB = Asian Development Bank, CO_2 = carbon dioxide, COVID-19 = coronavirus disease.
Source: Authors' analysis based on Transport DataBank (accessed 1 July 2020).

Figure 13: Satellite Images of Nitrogen Dioxide Emissions in the People's Republic of China, January–March 2020

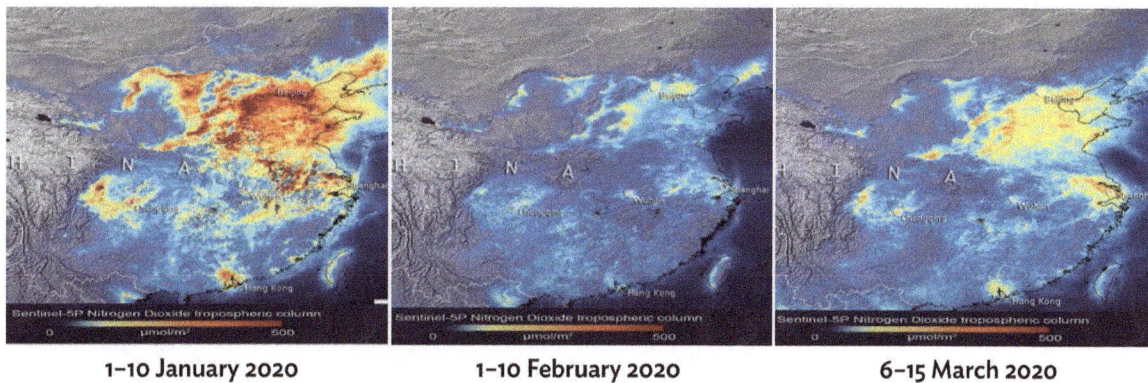

1–10 January 2020   1–10 February 2020   6–15 March 2020

Source: European Space Agency. 2020. COVID-19: Nitrogen Dioxide over China (accessed 11 May 2020).

Similar temporary improvements in air quality were observed in India, which recorded decreases of 43% for $PM_{2.5}$, 31% for PM_{10}, 10% for carbon monoxide, and 18% for NO_2 during 16 March–14 April 2020 compared with figures from previous years.[35] Table 3 shows that other cities in Southeast Asia also realized comparable improvements in air quality as a result of restrictions in transport and economic activity. However, as lockdowns are being relaxed and transport and economic demand are increasing slowly, air pollution is set to increase again.[36]

Table 3: Air Quality in Selected Asian Cities, March–April 2020

City	Changes in Nitrogen Dioxide Compared with Baseline (2015–2019) Levels (%)		
	1 March 2020	31 March 2020	17 April 2020
Bangkok	(1)	(21)	(22)
Ha Noi	(25)		
Ho Chi Minh City	3	(9)	1
Jakarta	(13)	(10)	(34)
Kuala Lumpur	(6)	(33)	(27)
Metro Manila	(5)	(31)	(34)
Phnom Penh	10	(4)	(6)
Singapore	(16)	(27)	(30)
Vientiane	(5)	0	(9)
Yangon	1	(4)	3

( ) = negative.
Source: K. Kanniah et al. 2020. COVID-19's Impact of the Atmospheric Environment of the Southeast Asia Region. *Science of The Total Environment*. 736. p. 139658.

Impact on Road Safety

In many countries, fewer people are traveling on roads because of the travel restrictions imposed to control the spread of COVID-19. Lower traffic on the roads is resulting in fewer road crashes. In France, the number of road accident casualties decreased by 40% and the number of seriously injured people reduced by 44% year-on-year in March 2020. Similar trends have been observed in California, where the number of casualties and seriously injured persons related to road accidents dropped by 50%.[37] In Asia too, the reduction in road travel has had a positive impact on road safety—but, as the example of Malaysia shows, the lifting of the lockdown will result in a rapid return to business as usual (Table 4).

Impact on the Economy

Transport is a key sector in most Asia and the Pacific economies. The transport sector's gross value added in ADB members is estimated to be $2.8 trillion, or about 4% of gross domestic product (GDP). Data from the International Labour Organization indicate that about 157 million people are employed in the transport industry in ADB members, of which 52% are in road and railway transport services (including pipelines) and 17% are in wholesale and retail trade and automobile repair (Figure 14).[38]

---

35 S. Sharma et al. 2020. Effect of Restricted Emissions during COVID-19 on Air Quality in India. *Science of The Total Environment*. 728. p. 138878.

36 A. Kumar, J. Burston, and J. Karliner. 2020. The Deadly Link between COVID-19 and Air Pollution. *World Economic Forum*. 15 April.

37 International Transport Forum. Re-Spacing Our Cities for Resilience. *COVID-19 Transport Brief*. 3 May.

38 International Labour Organization. ILOSTAT Database (accessed 20 June 2020).

Table 4: Road Safety Impact Examples of COVID-19 Restrictions for Selected Asian Countries

Country	Road Accidents
India[a]	The absolute number of road accidents declined but accident fatality rates increased because of increased speed.
Malaysia[b]	The partial lifting of lockdown resulted in a rapid increase in road accidents compared with the full lockdown period.
Thailand[c]	The number of road accidents dropped by 13% in May because of the stay-at-home policy during the COVID-19 pandemic lockdown.
Viet Nam[d]	Because of pandemic restrictions, the road accident cases in the country saw a year-on-year fall of nearly 14%.

COVID-19 = coronavirus disease.
[a] *Livemint.* 2020. Covid-19 Lockdown: 140 Deaths due to Road Accidents during March 24–May 3, Says Report. 6 May.
[b] J. Kaos, Jr. and F. Zainal. 2020. "Road Accidents Soar during CMCO" says Malaysia Health Ministry. *AsiaOne.* 11 June.
[c] *Xinhua.* 2020. Road Accidents in Thailand Drop by 13 pct in May due to COVID-19 Lockdown. 23 June.
[d] D. Khoa. 2020. COVID-19 Drives down Vietnam's Traffic Accidents. *VNExpress.* 6 April.
Source: Compiled by the Asian Development Bank.

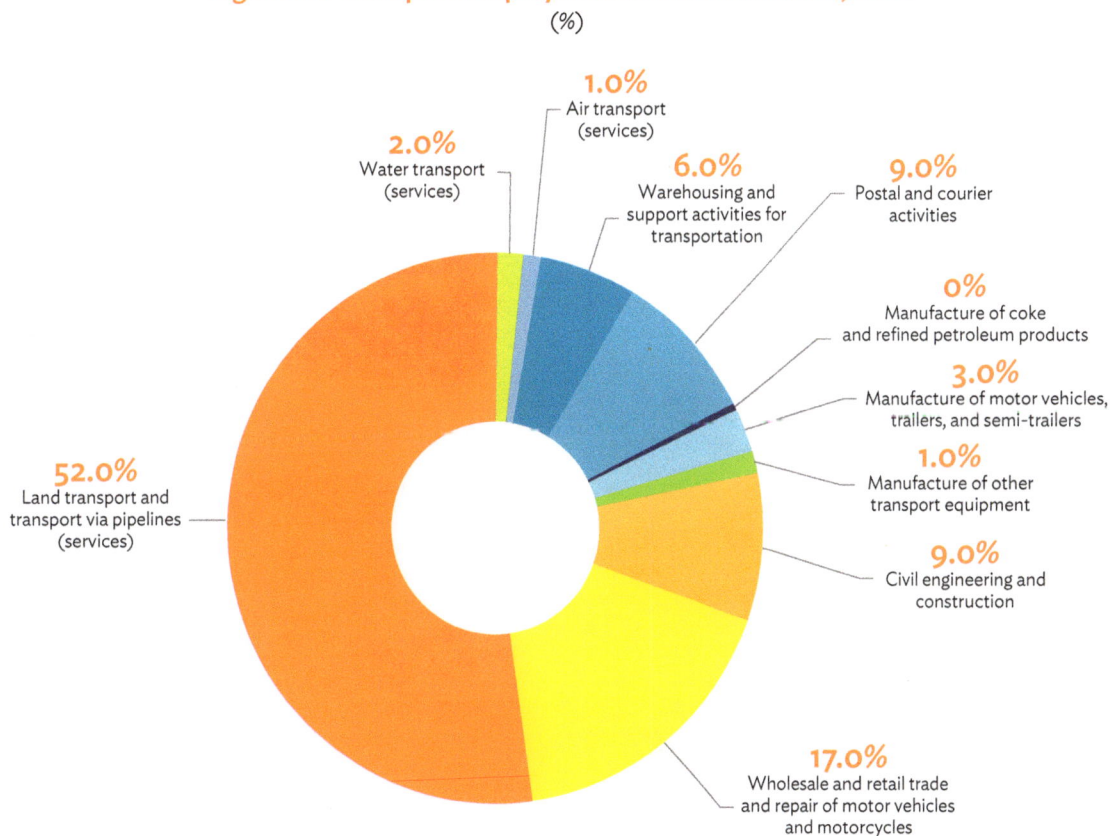

Figure 14: Transport Employment in ADB Members, 2020
(%)

- 1.0% Air transport (services)
- 2.0% Water transport (services)
- 6.0% Warehousing and support activities for transportation
- 9.0% Postal and courier activities
- 0% Manufacture of coke and refined petroleum products
- 3.0% Manufacture of motor vehicles, trailers, and semi-trailers
- 1.0% Manufacture of other transport equipment
- 9.0% Civil engineering and construction
- 52.0% Land transport and transport via pipelines (services)
- 17.0% Wholesale and retail trade and repair of motor vehicles and motorcycles

ADB = Asian Development Bank.
Source: Authors' analysis based on International Labour Organization data.

Initial assessment suggests the transport sector is particularly vulnerable in economies where it makes a significant contribution to GDP and employment, such as Cambodia, Fiji, the Lao People's Democratic Republic, Maldives, Sri Lanka, Thailand, and Viet Nam (Table 5).

Table 5: Impact of COVID-19 on Transport Services-Related Gross Domestic Product and Employment for Selected ADB Members

ADB member	As % of Transport Services GDP			As % of Transport Services Employment		
	Short Impact	Large Impact	Significant Outbreak	Short Impact	Large Impact	Significant Outbreak
Australia	(6.47)	(13.82)		(7.22)	(15.29)	
Bangladesh	(0.1)	(0.24)	(3.33)	(0.1)	(0.23)	(3.32)
Bhutan	(0.8)	(1.62)	(3.86)	(0.91)	(1.81)	(3.81)
Brunei Darussalam	(2.27)	(4.68)	(4.07)	(2.53)	(5.27)	(4.64)
Cambodia	(20.72)	(41.71)	(33.07)	(20.72)	(41.71)	(33.07)
Fiji	(9.43)	(19.4)	(15.37)	(7.48)	(15.4)	(12.57)
Hong Kong, China	(11.49)	(22.82)	(18.25)	(11.23)	(22.3)	(17.86)
India	(0.66)	(1.35)	(4.05)	(0.44)	(0.91)	(3.76)
Indonesia	(0.62)	(1.23)	(4.26)	(0.51)	(1.01)	(4.08)
Japan	(3.8)	(8.58)		(3.29)	(7.64)	
Kazakhstan	(2.61)	(5.27)	(6.44)	(1.49)	(3.05)	(4.65)
Kyrgyz Republic	(12.91)	(25.82)	(21.84)	(5.51)	(11.03)	(10.75)
Lao PDR	(12.08)	(24.26)	(20.31)	(4.91)	(9.89)	(9.67)
Malaysia	(3.18)	(6.42)	(6.56)	(3.02)	(6.1)	(6.33)
Maldives	(18.91)	(38.25)	(29.65)	(12.25)	(24.82)	(19.54)
Mongolia	(5.37)	(9.75)	(9.55)	(6.05)	(11.02)	(10.46)
Nepal	(1.46)	(2.95)	(5.37)	(0.87)	(1.82)	(3.57)
Pakistan	(0.08)	(0.17)	(3.83)	(0.11)	(0.25)	(3.8)
PRC	(5.31)	(6.76)		(5.22)	(6.53)	
Philippines	(1.68)	(3.42)	(5.36)	(1.65)	(3.36)	(5.34)
Republic of Korea	(3.75)	(8.08)		(4.9)	(10.25)	
Singapore	(6.38)	(12.75)	(10.39)	(6.41)	(12.81)	(10.43)
Sri Lanka	(5.69)	(11.53)	(11.55)	(5.69)	(11.53)	(11.55)
Taipei,China	(5.44)	(10.88)	(9.6)	(5.39)	(10.79)	(9.39)
Thailand	(8.85)	(17.8)	(15)	(8.12)	(16.33)	(13.88)
Viet Nam	(7.01)	(14.17)	(12.05)	(6.87)	(13.86)	(11.95)

( ) = negative, ADB = Asian Development Bank, COVID-19 = coronavirus disease, GDP = gross domestic product, Lao PDR = Lao People's Democratic Republic, PRC = People's Republic of China.
Source: ADB Data Library. COVID-19 Economic Impact Assessment Template (accessed 20 June 2020).

Figure 15 illustrates that the transport sector is particularly vulnerable to economic shocks induced by COVID-19. The impact could be much longer than the duration of the health emergency. The predicted economic slowdown and recession could further challenge the development of transport infrastructure, services, investments, and innovation and technologies among different modes.

Unlike some other economic sectors, in the transport sector, COVID-19 will affect employment (Figure 15). Automotive manufacturing has received much of the attention, especially in the context of economic stimulus packages in Europe. Yet in Asia, the number of jobs at risk in automobile manufacturing is modest (about 1 million) compared with the overall number of people employed in the transport sector (152 million), as Table 6 shows.

Figure 15: COVID-19 Gross Domestic Product and Employment Impact by Economic Sector in ADB Members

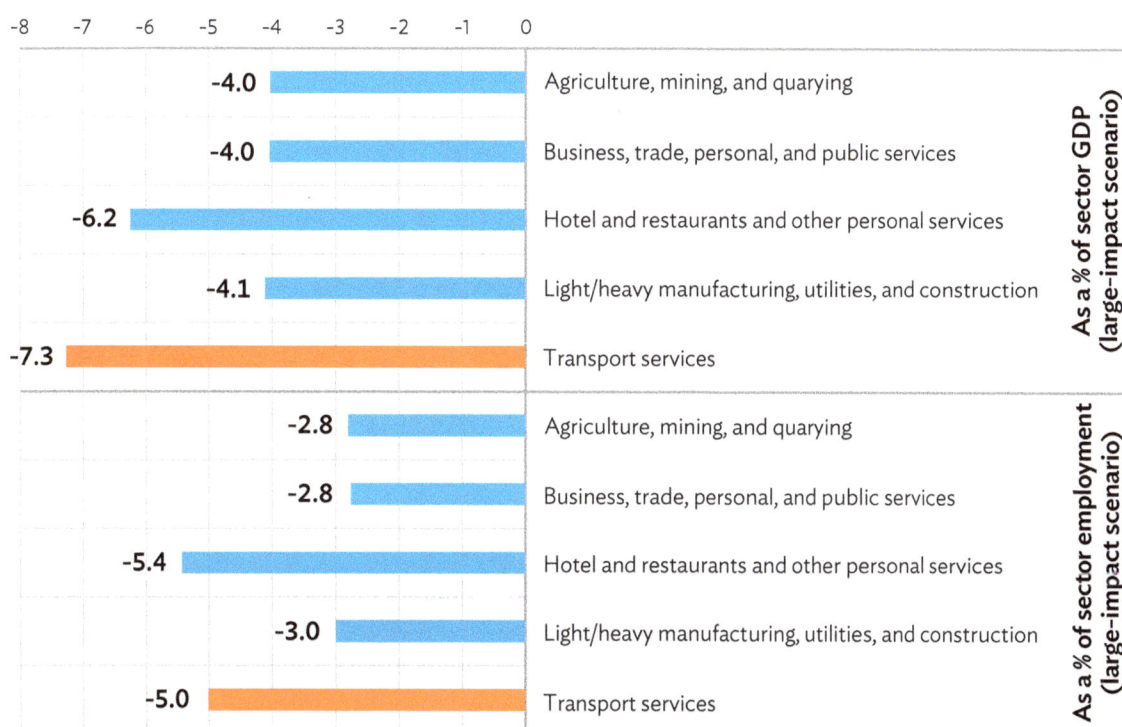

	-8	-7	-6	-5	-4	-3	-2	-1	0	

As a % of sector GDP (large-impact scenario)
- -4.0 Agriculture, mining, and quarrying
- -4.0 Business, trade, personal, and public services
- -6.2 Hotel and restaurants and other personal services
- -4.1 Light/heavy manufacturing, utilities, and construction
- -7.3 Transport services

As a % of sector employment (large-impact scenario)
- -2.8 Agriculture, mining, and quarrying
- -2.8 Business, trade, personal, and public services
- -5.4 Hotel and restaurants and other personal services
- -3.0 Light/heavy manufacturing, utilities, and construction
- -5.0 Transport services

ADB = Asian Development Bank, COVID-19 = coronavirus disease, GDP = gross domestic product.
Notes:
[1] The values are weighted averages for the large-impact scenario.
[2] The ADB members include Australia; Bangladesh; Bhutan; Brunei Darussalam; Cambodia; Fiji; Hong Kong, China; India; Indonesia; Japan; Kazakhstan; the Kyrgyz Republic; the Lao People's Democratic Republic; Malaysia; Maldives; Mongolia; Nepal; Pakistan; the People's Republic of China; the Philippines; the Republic of Korea; Singapore; Sri Lanka; Taipei,China; Thailand; and Viet Nam.
Source: ADB Data Library. COVID-19 Economic Impact Assessment Template.

Table 6: Impact of COVID-19 on Car Production and Automotive-Related Employment

Country or Region	Car Production in 2019 (million)	Jobs in 2019 (million)	Jobs at Risk (million)
People's Republic of China	22.6	4.3	0.6
Europe	21.8	3.8	0.5
United States	15.5	2.2	0.3
Southeast Asia[a]	13.8	1.9	0.3
Latin America	3.9	0.7	0.1
India	3.6	0.7	0.1
Other regions[b]	2.9	0.5	0.1
Africa	1.1	0.2	0.0

COVID-19 = coronavirus disease.

[a] Southeast Asia includes Brunei Darussalam, Cambodia, Indonesia, the Lao People's Democratic Republic, Malaysia, Myanmar, the Philippines, Singapore, Thailand, and Viet Nam.

[b] "Other regions" are defined to include the Middle East and Caribbean regions.

Source: International Energy Agency. 2020. *World Energy Outlook Special Report: A Sustainable Recovery*. Paris.

3 Exit Strategy for Lockdown

Successive lockdowns around the world have caused a collapse in global demand and supply of goods and services. The impacts of these lockdowns are being felt at all levels, from individual job security to the global economy and trade. Experts believe there may not be a return to normalcy until a vaccine is found and disseminated widely. The timeline is uncertain and could be more than a year. In the meantime, countries should expect to enter a stage of coexistence with the virus. A pattern of intermittent easing and tightening of restrictions in the coming months may be likely, to keep new infections under control while balancing a rebooted economy.

Figure 16 describes four trends that could characterize the development of the transport sector in Asia as it emerges from the pandemic. The actual scenario is likely to be a combination of the four trends and will differ between and possibly within economies. For example, demand for public transit is gradually recovering in ADB members Japan; Singapore; and Taipei,China—albeit at a slower pace compared with driving private vehicles (Appendix 3). Precautionary protective measures are in place to assure and enhance public transit users' confidence. Economic slowdown, sustained remote working, e-learning, and e-commerce are contributing to reduced travel demand. Developing economies, such as the Philippines and Thailand, are showing similar trends, with driving recovering faster than public transit ridership. On the other hand, India is experiencing a much faster recovery of public transit ridership than of driving, most likely because of a relatively higher proportion of captive users. In several developed cities in Europe, extensive government investment in cycling infrastructure has contributed to increased uptake of walking and cycling.

Figure 16: Possible Post-COVID-19 Trends for the Transport Sector in ADB Members

TREND 1 Demand returns for public transport

Demand for public transport returns to pre-pandemic levels.

Factors:
- ◆ The virus is under control and there is no reason to avoid public transport.

Or:
- ◆ Staying home is not an option for economic reasons.
- ◆ There is a high proportion of captive users on public transport.
- ◆ There is a lack of viable alternatives (e.g., absence of nonmotorized transport, facilities, and connectivity).

TREND 3 Private transport (car and motorcycle) is king

There is unwillingness to return to public transport. Private transport is preferred.

Factors:
- ◆ There is lack of public confidence in public transport (health concerns).
- ◆ Users can afford to switch to other modes (e.g., private cars or motorcycles).
- ◆ Walking and cycling are not seen as adequate alternatives.

TREND 2 Shifts to active transport mode (walk and cycle)

Travel mode shifts to walking, cycling, and 2–3 wheelers. There is less reliance on public transport. Private car mode may hold, or be slightly suppressed through road space reallocation.

Factors:
- ◆ Safe and viable alternatives of nonmotorized transport modes are available.
- ◆ Road space is reallocated for nonmotorized transport modes.

TREND 4 Decreased travel demand

Work-from-home and e-commerce, and/or economic recession, result in an overall lower frequency of travel.

Factors:
- ◆ Economic downturn reduces demand for passenger and freight transport.
- ◆ There is reasonably high level of digital inclusion and literacy (e.g., availability of digital infrastructure and services).
- ◆ E-commerce penetration is high.
- ◆ The types of occupations allow commuters to work remotely.

ADB = Asian Development Bank, COVID-19 = coronavirus disease.
Source: ADB.

A consumer survey by the Boston Consulting Group of 5,200 urban residents in the EU, the PRC, and the US reveals early signs of changing consumer preferences in transport mode choices (Figure 17). Initial indications are that consumers in the PRC prefer to use private modes of transport (such as cars, bicycles, or new-mobility devices such as shared bicycles or scooters) over public transit. The propensity to switch to driving is higher for the higher-income group. It should be remembered, however, that several of the largest cities in the PRC have vehicle quotas in place, which suppressed demand for personal cars before the pandemic. Several cities in the PRC have announced temporary relaxations of these vehicle quotas, especially for "new energy vehicles" and cars manufactured in the concerned city or province.[39] Similar surveys carried out by other agencies indicate a high propensity to switch to driving among noncaptive public transit users.[40]

---

[39] *Gasgoo China Automotive News.* 2020. China's Automobile Industry Policy Updates – May 2020. 2 June.
[40] J. Zhang and Y. Hayashi. 2020. Impacts of COVID-19 on the Transport Sector and Measures as well as Recommendations of Policies and Future Research: Analyses Based on a World-Wide Expert Survey. *SSRN.* 7 June.

Figure 17: Anticipated Changes in Consumer Spending on Urban Transport in the European Union, the People's Republic of China, and the United States

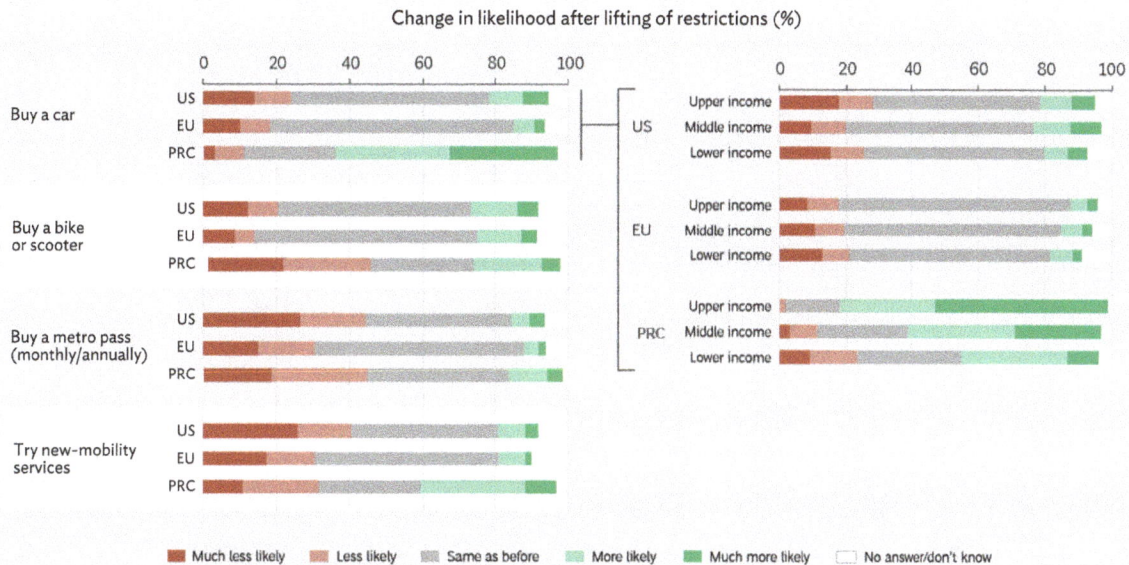

Change in likelihood after lifting of restrictions (%)

Much less likely | **Less likely** | **Same as before** | **More likely** | **Much more likely** | No answer/don't know

EU = European Union, PRC = People's Republic of China, US = United States.
Note: The survey polled 5,200 urban residents in these three countries.
Source: J. Bert et al. 2020. How COVID-19 Will Shape Urban Mobility. *Boston Consulting Group*. 16 June.

Economic Stimulus for the Transport Sector

Economies in the developed world have enacted unprecedented financial support packages. The transport sector is benefiting from this through financial support to subsectors such as the airline industry, automotive, and public transit companies. There is an ongoing discussion on whether and how financial support can be linked to decarbonization and sustainable development criteria.[41] The International Energy Agency has issued a special report on a sustainable recovery, which points out that the employment multiplier (jobs per unit of investment) for the automotive sector is low compared with investment in walking and cycling infrastructure and charging facilities (Figure 18). The International Labour Organization and the United Nations Economic Commission for Europe estimate that increasing investment in public transit and electric vehicles could create at least 15 million new jobs globally.[42]

---

[41] For example, International Energy Agency. 2020. *World Energy Outlook Special Report: A Sustainable Recovery*. Paris.
[42] International Labour Organization and United Nations Economic Commission for Europe. 2020. *Jobs in Green and Healthy Transport: Making the Green Shift*. Geneva.

Figure 18: Employment Multipliers for Investment in the Transport Sector
(jobs per $ million)

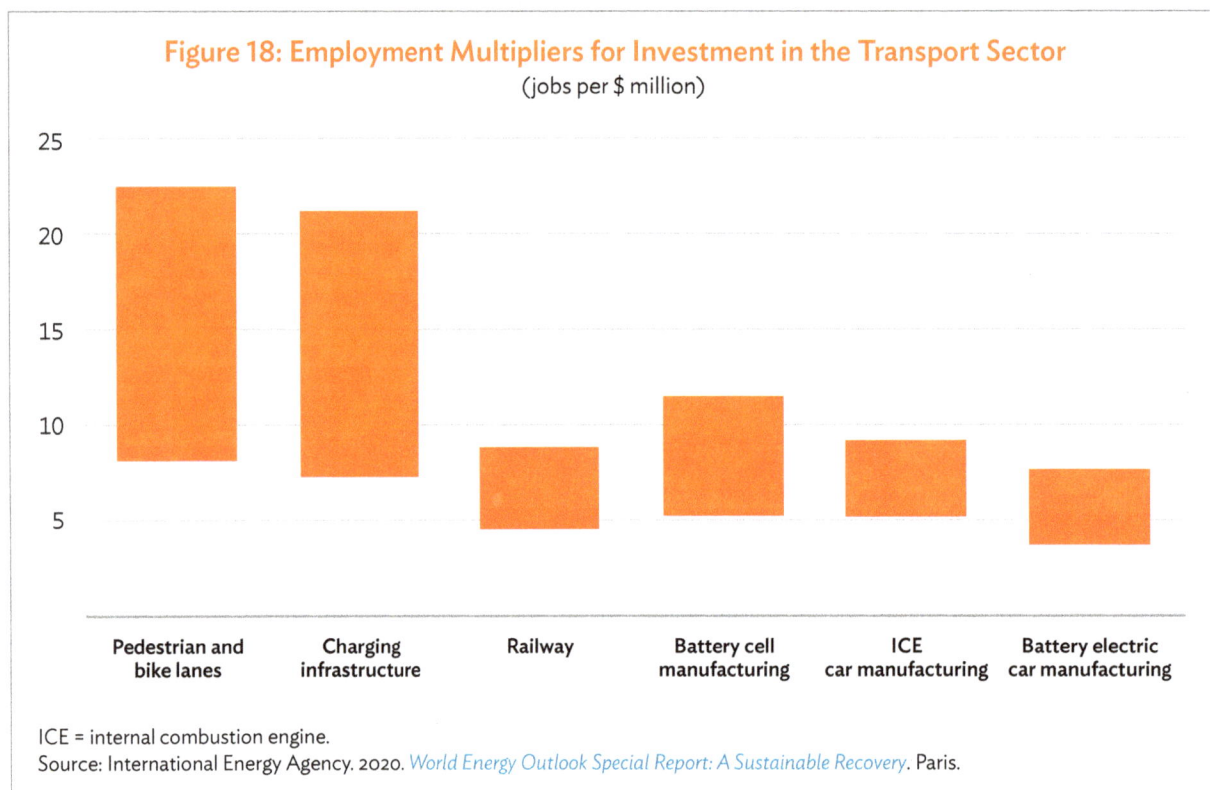

ICE = internal combustion engine.
Source: International Energy Agency. 2020. *World Energy Outlook Special Report: A Sustainable Recovery*. Paris.

Economies in Asia and the Pacific may not have the possibilities to enact similar types of economic support packages but several of them are taking measures to support transport-related industries. This includes support to the aviation sector, automotive, and public transit and transport infrastructure (Table 7). It is expected that, in the coming weeks and months, other economies will announce further support measures.

Table 7: Examples of Transport-Related Stimulus Measures in ADB Members

ADB Member	Example
Bhutan[a]	The fiscal stimulus includes implementation of an economic contingency plan aimed at helping different sectors, including farm road infrastructure construction.
Fiji[b]	The Government of Fiji has allocated $200 million to Fiji Airways to reduce the economic impact caused by the COVID-19 crisis.
Georgia[c]	The Government of Georgia has insured the construction materials for all infrastructure projects against price spikes (GEL200 million).
Hong Kong, China[d]	The Hong Kong Airport Authority has rolled out a HK$1 billion package of financial relief to the aviation industry. The package includes a government waiver of air traffic control charges and airport fee relief for airlines and airport users. For the passenger transport segment, the stimulus includes a monthly subsidy of HK$6,000 for 6 months to each eligible active taxi and red minibus driver; a one-off subsidy of HK$30,000 for the registered owner of each taxi, red minibus, nonfranchised bus, school private light bus, and hire car; and reimbursement of 100% of the actual regular repair and maintenance costs and insurance premium for 6 months for the five franchised bus companies, nine franchised/licensed ferry operators, and Hong Kong Tramways Limited.

continued on next page

Table 7 *continued*

ADB Member	Example
Indonesia[e]	The Government of Indonesia is reducing income tax by 30% for businesses in 19 selected manufacturing industries, including motor vehicle, trailer, and semitrailer manufacturers. The government will also provide an estimated Rp10 trillion in incentives for the tourism industry, including airlines and travel agents. The incentives are in the form of airline ticket discounts to the 10 priority domestic tourism destinations and discounts on airplane fuel provided by Pertamina.
Malaysia[f]	The Economic Stimulus Package of RM20 billion is to encourage domestic tourism to boost demand for public transport. Public transport operators, especially in the aviation and railway sectors, will benefit from the allocation of up toRM100 in digital vouchers per person for domestic flights, rail transport, and hotel accommodation.
People's Republic of China[g]	The PRC has revised its new energy vehicle credit score program for 2021–2023 and has extended credit targets to 14% in 2021, 16% in 2022, and 18% in 2023. It has also extended a waiver on port construction fees for imported and exported cargoes from 30 June 2020 to 31 December 2020.
Philippines[h]	The Department of Transportation is pushing for the passage of the Philippine Economic Stimulus Act 2020 to provide immediate financial assistance to workers and businesses affected by the pandemic.
Republic of Korea[i]	The Government of the Republic of Korea has deferred payments for airport landing, parking, and facility fees. State-run banks have also agreed to provide unsecured loans worth W300 billion to help low-cost airlines. The incentives may also include a proposal for a 30%–50% aircraft property tax reduction for major airlines and government purchasing of stakes involved in public infrastructure. Some of the incentives for auto industry include faster customs clearance, and freight transportation and liquidity support for the automobile industry.
Singapore[j]	On 26 March 2020, Singapore initiated measures to help aviation and other sectors. Measures include funding 75% of up to S$4,600 of aviation workers' monthly pay and providing S$350 million in fee relief for airlines. This is part of a massive S$48 billion economic stimulus package announced by the government.
Viet Nam[k]	To stimulate automotive sales, the Government of Viet Nam is planning to reduce vehicle registration fees by 50% until the end of the year. It is also planning to remove import tariffs for auto parts and accessories that currently cannot be manufactured domestically.

$ = United States dollar, ADB = Asian Development Bank, COVID-19 = coronavirus disease, GEL = Georgian lari, HK$ = Hong Kong dollar, PRC = People's Republic of China, RM = ringgit, Rp = rupiah, S$ = Singapore dollar, W = won.

[a] International Monetary Fund. Policy Responses to COVID-19 (accessed 20 June 2020).
[b] *RNZ*. 2020. Fiji Airways Gets Govt Support to Stay Afloat. 27 May.
[c] K. Rukhadze. 2020. Georgia Government and Institution Measures in Response to COVID-19. *KPMG*. 29 April.
[d] C. Ng, P. Cowley, and L. Wolfers. 2020. Hong Kong (SAR), China: Government and Institution Measures in Response to COVID-19. *KPMG*. 10 June.
[e] *ASEAN Briefing*. 2020. Indonesia Issues Second Stimulus Package to Dampen COVID-19 Impact. 18 March.
[f] T. Yusof. 2020. Stimulus Package a Boost for Public Transportation Sector. *New Straits Times*. 28 February.
[g] *Argus*. 2020. China Issues NEV Credit Scheme for 2021–2023. 22 June.
[h] E. Abadilla and A. D. San Juan. 2020. Transport Sector to get ₱70 billion from PESA. *Manila Bulletin*. 27 May.
[i] E. White and S. Jung-a. 2020. South Korea Boosts Coronavirus Crisis Stimulus Package to $200bn. *Financial Times*. 22 April; and *The Economic Times Auto.com*. 2020. South Korea to Help Auto Industry Ride Out Covid-19 Pandemic. 23 March.
[j] *Center for Aviation*. 2020. COVID-19: SIA Group the Big Winner in Asia Pac Bailouts. 30 March.
[k] A. Madhok. 2020. Weekly Update: COVID-19 Impact on Global Automotive Industry. *Counterpoint*. 15 September; and N. Thuy. 2020. Vietnam Takes New Tax Step to Stimulate Car Market. *Hanoi Times*. 29 May.
Source: Compiled by the Asian Development Bank.

Good Practices for Enhancing the Resilience of Transport Services

Policy makers, regulators, and especially transport operators can take several measures to enhance the health resilience of transport systems and reduce the likelihood of users becoming infected as lockdowns are eased. This is especially relevant during the phase when COVID-19 infections are declining but the risk of community transmission still exists. Once there is no longer a substantial chance of community transmission, the good practices listed on pp. 36–38 (under public transit, active transport, aviation, and freight and logistics), especially those on social distancing, are likely to be further relaxed or completely abandoned.

Public Transit

Public transit (including buses) plays an important role, particularly in densely populated cities. It provides the most efficient way of transporting large numbers of passengers in a cost-effective, affordable, and environmentally sustainable manner. Well-planned urban public transport systems also contribute to enhancing the accessibility and vibrancy of the city and quality of life for its residents.

However, under pandemic conditions, the physical nature of public transport—the close distance between passengers at the station and in the vehicle—inevitably creates conditions that promote viral transmission. Several countries, such as India and the Philippines, imposed the highest level of restrictions and lockdown.[43] Public transport operations, including taxis, shared mobility services, paratransit, and tricycles, ceased; all that was permitted was private movement through passenger cars, bicycles, and walking, and some types of food delivery vehicles. Other ADB members, such as the Republic of Korea; Singapore; and Taipei,China, allowed varying levels of economic activity. Public transport played a key role in enabling frontline workers to get to work.

With the benefit of hindsight, it has become clear that public transport systems could be kept open, with operations limited to essential workers in the health and other sectors, provided the necessary preventive measures are in place, combined with widespread testing, contact tracing, and health monitoring. The advice on safe distances in public transport has ranged between 1 and 2 meters. The larger the distances, the greater the impact on effective in-vehicle capacity. Figure 19 offers a possible configuration of reduced capacity by more than 75% on public transport with safe-distancing measures in place. These calculations are expected to vary depending on different capacity configurations (e.g., seats and standing). In the case illustrated, effective capacity may be reduced to one-quarter. In another words, to serve the same pre-pandemic passenger demand, the required capacity would have to be quadrupled, which would be financially challenging without some form of government subsidy. In practice, therefore, many public transport operators, guided by regulatory policy actions, are opting for less stringent social distancing combined with the compulsory use of masks in public transit stations and in public transit vehicles.

Asian cities, especially in developing countries, may be able to stagger ridership throughout during the day and across the transit system to reduce peak transit demand. However, enforcing such a transformation within a short period of time could be difficult, given land use patterns, trip behaviors, and poor access to limited transit systems.

---

[43] See Appendix 1 for a full overview of restrictions on public transport in Asian countries.

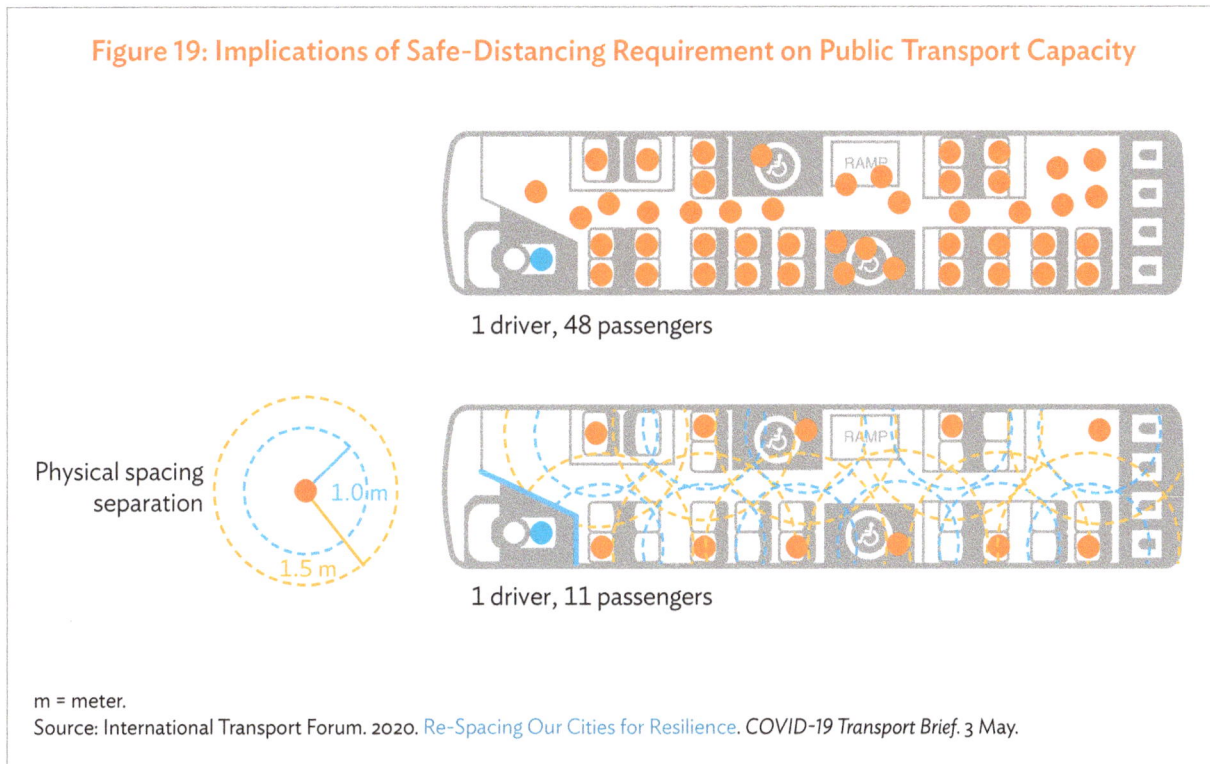

Figure 19: Implications of Safe-Distancing Requirement on Public Transport Capacity

1 driver, 48 passengers

Physical spacing separation

1.0 m

1.5 m

1 driver, 11 passengers

m = meter.

Source: International Transport Forum. 2020. Re-Spacing Our Cities for Resilience. *COVID-19 Transport Brief.* 3 May.

Demand for urban public transit during the pandemic has been suppressed and is expected to remain below pre-COVID-19 levels if work-from-home trends and e-learning are sustained. The two key challenges are (i) tackling capacity challenges on public transport in the context of safe-distancing requirements, and (ii) how best to regain public confidence to encourage a return to public transport. Additional efforts will be required to reassure public transport users of safety precautions and demonstrate that public transport is clean and safe. Government policies and financial support will be essential to enable public transport operators to remain viable so they can continue to support the movement of passengers and goods to keep the economy going while ensuring longer-term sustainability.

Active Transport—Walking and Cycling

Walking and cycling promote well-being and health. More crucially, they are far more environmentally friendly options, contributing to enhanced air quality, lower CO_2 emissions, and livability of cities. Active transport modes tend to offer a higher switching opportunity during change conditions such as the pandemic, as they provide a cost-effective alternative to meet safe-distancing requirements and relieve the burden on public transport.

Under pandemic conditions, active modes of transport have seen mixed results. In cases where a total lockdown was instituted, walking and cycling were no longer possible. In cases where lockdown restrictions were less strict, increases in walking and cycling were observed. Several cities across the world have urged their citizens to walk or cycle in order to reduce the risk of infection. As well as offering a viable option to ensure safe distancing, governments are promoting cycling to avoid dramatic shifts to private vehicles after the lockdowns are lifted.[44]

---

[44] N. Parveen and H. Pidd. 2020. Encourage Cycling and Walking after Lockdown, UK Mayors Told. *The Guardian.* 1 May.

Several cities in Europe, such as Berlin, Milan, and Paris, and in other parts of the world, such as Bogota and New York, have embarked on ambitious expansion plans to promote walking and cycling by reallocating existing public spaces and road space, and retrofitting them with semipermanent or permanent structures to enhance safe-distanced walking and cycling facilities quickly. Berlin was one of the first cities to have substantially expanded its cycle networks, in mid-March 2020. By June 2020, this practice had been replicated in more than 150 cities worldwide. Although such measures have increased bike usage, it is worth noting that such successes have tended to rely on an existing culture of bike riding in the city.[45]

Aviation—Passengers

Realistically, safe distancing can be achieved more easily during the passenger handling process for airport departures and arrivals. On aircrafts, safe distancing means leaving empty seats between passengers. According to IATA, such measures would reduce overall global seat capacity to 62%,[46] which is considerably lower than most airlines' break-even average load factor of 77%.[47] All else being equal, airfares would need to increase for airlines to break even, and this would be a challenge given weak demand in the short term. Regulators have permitted several airlines to ignore social distancing rules as long as masks are worn on the aircraft.

Freight and Logistics

While logistics operations seem less affected than passenger transport, there are major adjustments in this subsector as well. Since the COVID-19 crisis began, air cargo has been a vital partner in delivering essential medicines and medical equipment, and in keeping global supply chains functioning for time-sensitive goods and commodities. To cope with a capacity shortage, airlines have brought freighters out of storage and used aircraft more intensely. Passenger planes have also been adapted for all-cargo operations.[48]

The impact of COVID-19 on demand for freight and logistics is of great concern. A prolonged recovery from the pandemic will slow the global economy and decrease aggregate demand, which will have a knock-on financial impact on the logistics business. Furthermore, the potential risks from deglobalization could have long-run implications for global supply chains. The challenge is for public sector regulators and the private sector, including manufacturers and shipping companies, to adjust nimbly to the changing economic landscape, restructure, and emerge more resilient from the pandemic.

To meet the surge in demand for last-mile delivery, many delivery service providers have had to invest additional resources in upgrading their logistics network, recruiting additional staff, and obtaining protective equipment such as masks. To meet increased demand, some countries have relaxed regulations to allow taxis and private hire cars to fill the gap, given that demand for the core business of taxi services and car hire companies has declined sharply since the pandemic.[49] Delivery service providers have also introduced contactless delivery options in compliance with safe-distancing measures.

---

[45] N. Panozzo. 2020. Covid-19 Cycling Measures Tracker Released Today. *European Cyclists' Federation*. 16 June.

[46] Specific reductions in capacity would depend on variations of seat configuration on different aircraft.

[47] IATA. 2020. Social Distancing Would Make Most Airlines Financially Unviable. IATA Economics' Chart of the Week. 8 May.

[48] IATA. 2020. *Guidance for the Transport of Cargo and Mail on Aircraft Configured for the Carriage of Passengers*. 3rd ed. Montreal, Canada.

[49] C. Guan and C. Chan. 2020. Commentary: Has COVID-19 Made e-Commerce and Online Shopping the New Normal? *Channel News Asia*. 7 April.

"Bounce-Back" Strategy and Framework

Throughout the lockdown, although low demand hit transport services severely, it was critical to maintain the minimum level of service to ensure continued mobility of essential workers and goods while avoiding further spread of COVID-19. As countries and cities look to exit and recover from the lockdown, transport will continue to play an important enabling role to support the needs of the population and the economy throughout the stages of recovery. The key challenge ahead is to enable transport to serve its economic and social role while ensuring the safety of transport users and enhancing the resilience of transport systems so they are better prepared to respond to any future pandemic. The ongoing pandemic has highlighted the need for the sector to handle the response as a comprehensive health and economic issue.

ADB has developed a "bounce-back" strategy and framework to assist countries exiting lockdowns (Figure 20). The strategy covers three phases—response phase in the immediate term (up to 3 months), recovery phase in the medium term (up to 1 year), and rejuvenation phase in the longer term (after 1 year)—before a vaccine becomes widely available. In the case of repeated waves of transmission, countries may fall back into earlier phases, and the successive phases in the three-stage process repeat themselves. This is a stylized strategy and it is important to be aware that the actual response will vary between countries and cities as well as among different transport subsectors within countries and cities.

A range of mostly health-related measures suitable for each phase has been collated, drawing from the wide range of resources that have been produced at national levels and by international agencies. Readers are encouraged to refer to detailed guidelines and references in Appendix 5. This chapter includes only a selection of the key measures, guiding principles, and good practices. The measures summarized here focus on operations in the different transport subsectors and do not deal with possible economic stimulus packages described in the first part of this chapter.

Figure 20: Bounce-Back Strategy to Exit a Lockdown

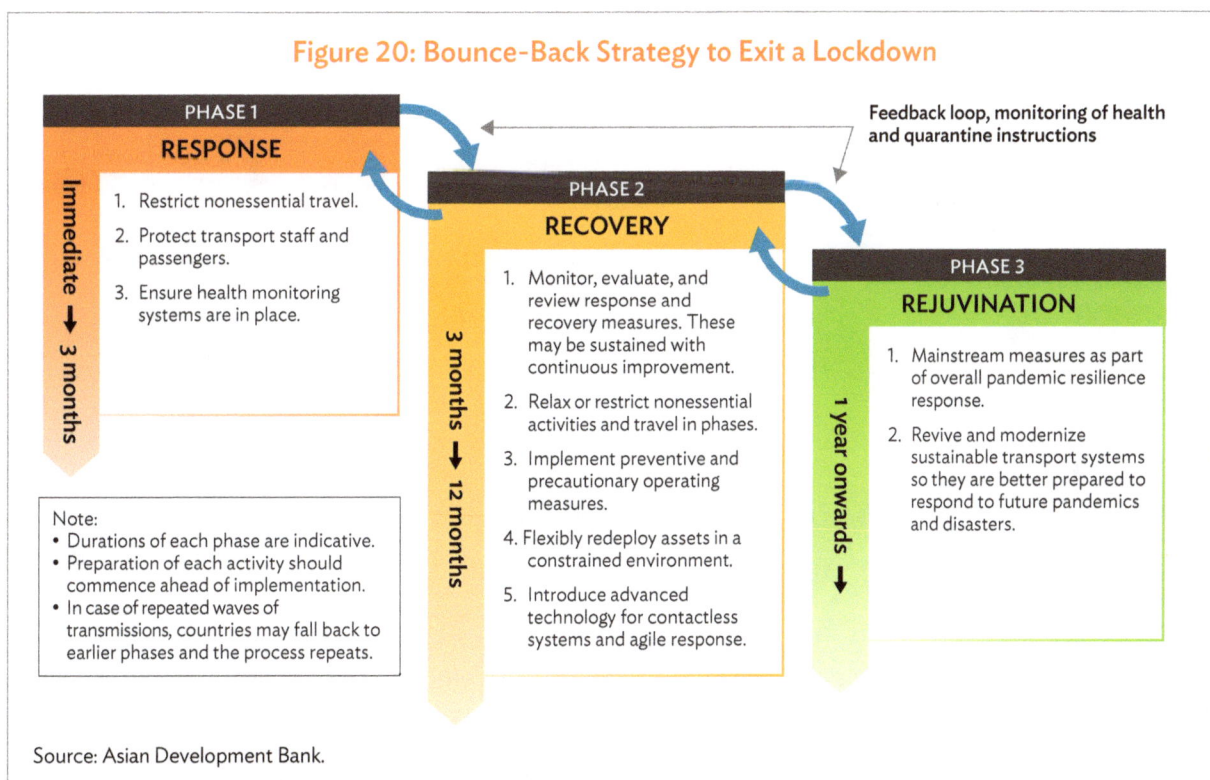

PHASE 1

RESPONSE

Immediate → 3 months

1. Restrict nonessential travel.
2. Protect transport staff and passengers.
3. Ensure health monitoring systems are in place.

Note:
- Durations of each phase are indicative.
- Preparation of each activity should commence ahead of implementation.
- In case of repeated waves of transmissions, countries may fall back to earlier phases and the process repeats.

PHASE 2

RECOVERY

3 months → 12 months

1. Monitor, evaluate, and review response and recovery measures. These may be sustained with continuous improvement.
2. Relax or restrict nonessential activities and travel in phases.
3. Implement preventive and precautionary operating measures.
4. Flexibly redeploy assets in a constrained environment.
5. Introduce advanced technology for contactless systems and agile response.

Feedback loop, monitoring of health and quarantine instructions

PHASE 3

REJUVINATION

1 year onwards →

1. Mainstream measures as part of overall pandemic resilience response.
2. Revive and modernize sustainable transport systems so they are better prepared to respond to future pandemics and disasters.

Source: Asian Development Bank.

In the immediate term, nonessential travel is still expected to be limited. The response phase focuses mainly on protecting transport staff and passengers, providing adequate protective equipment (including personal protective equipment, gloves, and masks), and enforcing new safety requirements. The frequency of cleaning and sanitization of common and shared facilities should be stepped up. Preventive measures should be put in place to implement safe-distancing requirements. Timely updates should be provided to staff and passengers, including on new infections and changes in public transit service frequencies and routes. Complementing these measures, it would be ideal to put in place a robust system of contact tracing and health monitoring before reopening. This can also enable authorities to monitor the risk level and rate of transmission, allowing agile responses to further restrict or relax movement as necessary. Table 8 provides a matrix of proposed response measures by transport mode.

When health conditions have improved and the risk of community transmission is declining, the second phase of measures may be considered. This involves monitoring, evaluating, and reviewing the response and recovery measures in tandem with health conditions and risks of transmission. Nonessential travel may be relaxed depending on the health situation.

Table 8: Proposed Response Measures by Transport Mode

Measures	Public Transit	Active Transport (Walking and Cycling)	National Roads	International Travel (Aviation)	Freight and Logistics
Restrict nonessential travel.	Control allowable movement and travel according to risk level of infections. Update regularly and adjust as required.				
Provide adequate protective equipment.	Ensure adequate supply of masks, personal protective equipment, and disinfection equipment.				
Protect transport staff.	Provide training, timely information, protective equipment, and preventive measures.			Provide training, timely information, protective equipment, and preventive measures.	
Protect passengers and consumers.	Provide timely information, implement and enforce preventive measures, and reconfigure passenger flows.	Provide timely information and implement and enforce preventive measures.		Provide timely information, implement and enforce preventive measures, and reconfigure passenger flows.	Enhance disinfection and sanitization regime of goods wherever relevant.
Protect infrastructure.	Enhance disinfection and sanitization regime of property and facilities.			Enhance disinfection and sanitization regime of property and facilities.	
Institute contact tracing.	Ensure contact tracing capability is in place to track transmission.				
Institute health monitoring.	Ensure health monitoring system is in place to make informed decision on relaxing and restricting movement.				

Source: Asian Development Bank.

At the time of writing, it appears domestic transport travel restrictions tend to be relaxed first, while restrictions on international travel are retained for longer for fear of external reintroduction of the virus. The "green lane" (e.g., in the PRC) and the "flight bubble" (e.g., in Australia and New Zealand) concepts are being applied as countries cautiously reopen international borders to passengers and cargo. For cargo movement, this calls for streamlined measures to establish dedicated lanes for freight vehicles and coordinate travel restrictions across borders to remove duplicative processes. For passenger movement, the cautious approach to reopening includes ensuring equivalent low levels of transmission of countries on both sides, and initially allowing only essential travel. In the case of Singapore, such decisions have been built on mutual cooperation with countries on common safeguards and coordination of quarantine orders to avoid passengers requiring multiple tests and quarantine.[50]

In the recovery phase, further preventive and precautionary operating measures and the introduction of advanced technology should also be implemented to enable contactless processes and facilitate an agile response (Table 9). Demand management measures can facilitate crowd control on public transit systems and in airports. As a complementary measure, capacity for walking and cycling could be scaled up to absorb spillover demand from public transit. To cope with lower and uncertain travel demand for public transit, aviation, and certain strategic freight routes, it is critical to assess whether restructuring or subsidies for concessions or service agreements are required to ensure essential transport links are kept open and core transport and freight operators remain financially viable.

Table 9: Proposed Recovery Measures by Transport Mode

Measures	Public Transit	Active Transport (Walking and Cycling)	National Roads	International Travel (Aviation)	Freight and Logistics
Introduce demand management measures.	Implement crowd-monitoring systems and adjust service frequencies to real-time demand.	Scale up nonmotorized transport capacity to absorb demand and improve safety and promote walking and cycling.		As a crowd control measure, apply an appointment system for embarkation processes.	
Introduce contactless technology.	Introduce contactless payment modes.			Implement contactless systems for embarkation and disembarkation.	Implement contactless payment and delivery for small parcel and last-mile deliveries.
Enhance safety.		Enhance road safety through physical and nonphysical measures to protect vulnerable users.			
Restructure concession and service agreements.	Review risk allocation and structure of agreements to enable operators to stay viable. Explore short-term service contract with operator.			Maintain adequate air connectivity through incentive programs or as part of financial bailout programs.	Explore concession and service agreements with air cargo services to ensure uninterrupted supply chains.
Provide financial subsidies.	Provide bridging loans to assist operators with cash flows and credit lines.	Provide subsidies for cycle purchase and repair.		Provide bridging loans to assist airlines with cash flows and credit lines.	Provide bridging loans to assist key logistics providers with required cash flows and credit lines.

continued on next page

50 T. Goh. 2020. Singapore in Discussions with S. Korea, Australia, to Establish "Green Lanes" for Travel. *The Straits Times*. 30 May.

Table 9 *continued*

Measures	Public Transit	Active Transport (Walking and Cycling)	National Roads	International Travel (Aviation)	Freight and Logistics
Relax or restrict nonessential travel in phases.	Promote work-from-home arrangements, staggered work and school shifts, e-commerce, and e-learning.			Employ the "travel bubble" concept.	Employ the "green lane" concept. Establish a regional cooperation body to coordinate travel restrictions across borders.
Monitor, review, and evaluate effectiveness of the response and recovery plan.	Continuously monitor, evaluate, and improve response measures, with incorporation of additional preventive measures.				
Explore alternative physical reconfiguration to mitigate the impact of safe distancing.	Introduce preventive health measures (e.g., health checks, database for travelers, and QR codes).			Introduce preventive health measures (e.g., health checks, database for travelers, and QR codes).	
Control transmission.	Health screening			Health screening, declarations, controls.	Enhanced screening on import and export cargo at border crossing points.
Flexibly redeploy assets in a constrained environment.	Adopt flexi-use of underutilized vehicles and services (e.g., taxis to transport essential workers).	Adopt flexi-use of underutilized nonmotorized transport and paratransit to supplement public transport services.	Reallocate road space for expanded nonmotorized transport capacity and/or emergency lanes for first responders.	Repurpose passenger planes for cargo operations to transport essential and/or emergency supplies.	Repurpose underutilized passenger planes to meet capacity shortfall in essential cargo.

Source: Asian Development Bank.

With further improvements in health conditions, the third phase involves mainstreaming measures in standard operating procedures. This will result in more resilient transport systems that are better prepared to respond to any future pandemic or disaster. The introduction of advanced technologies to enable digitalizing and contactless systems during the response and recovery phases would lay the foundations for further transformative changes in the long term. At this stage, efforts should also be made to broaden digital inclusion to realize the full benefits of more integrated and agile systems. Table 10 provides a matrix of proposed rejuvenation measures by transport mode.

Table 10: Proposed Rejuvenation Measures by Transport Mode

Measures	Public Transit	Active Transport (Walking and Cycling)	National Roads	International Travel (Aviation)	Freight and Logistics
Enhance long-term sustainability of services and assets.	Develop financing structures for adjusted service plan catering to reduced post-lockdown demand.		Continue to improve road safety and road maintenance for all users.	Explore restructuring of aviation industry to share demand risks appropriately between the public and private sectors.	Restructure the logistics supply chain to enhance resilience.
Mainstream measures as part of overall pandemic-resilient response and operations plan.	Mainstream contactless payment and systems.	Mainstream temporary measures to expand capacity for walking, cycling, and emergency services in future pandemic response and operations plan.	Mainstream temporary traffic measures in road design standards to accommodate permanent or temporary increased capacity for nonmotorized transport or emergency lanes.	Mainstream contactless processes and systems for embarking and disembarking for international travel.	
	Develop integrated transport masterplan (temporary measures) across modes as part of a pandemic response and operations plan.				
				Pending support from medical evidence, explore applicability of "immunity passports."	
Institute transformative change.	Integrate contactless payment with other e-payment platforms.			Further develop contactless and digital systems for embarking and disembarking for transformative change.	Integrate digital platforms to facilitate e-commerce and urban logistics.
	Explore mobility as a service.				Explore mobility as a service for last-mile delivery.

Source: Asian Development Bank.

A more detailed description of measures for each transport subsector is in Appendix 4. The success of preventive measures also relies on citizens to act in a socially responsible manner, which may require behavioral changes. It may be months before handshakes and friendly hugs return as the norm in social settings.

4 The Transport Sector after COVID-19

COVID-19 has put the transport sector in Asia and the Pacific in an extraordinary situation as the sector has been caught up in a big way in the public health, economic, and humanitarian crisis that has arisen across the continent. Substantial work lies ahead for all transport stakeholders—including governments, the private sector, citizens, and development partners—to work together to navigate a way out of this crisis in an environment of tremendous uncertainty and high stakes.

The pandemic has struck at a time of ongoing global challenges in Asia and the Pacific, such as climate change, an aging population, and rural–urban migration. Drastic behavioral and lifestyle changes have been adopted on a global scale almost overnight. This has shifted the way we work and live, and has consequently redefined our transport needs and posed a new and complex array of challenges. The disruption and associated uncertainty can bring about significant change, and a pressing question is whether this represents a new normal or whether the transport sector will rebound to "business as usual."

In deciding the future of transport in Asia and the Pacific, it will be important to combine the pre-pandemic agenda as framed by the Sustainable Development Goals, the Paris Agreement, and other international agreements, and ADB's Strategy 2030, with the specific implications of the COVID-19 pandemic. This may require some rethinking of the solutions needed to improve transport in Asia and the Pacific. Transport policy is becoming increasingly complex, owing to the development issues of integrating across different sectors and thematic areas, different modes of transport, transport management, cross-border flow of goods and people, planning and financing, and the need to improve inclusivity for the wide range of users and stakeholders.

The future of the transport sector post COVID-19 will be heavily influenced by how long and deep the economic recession is globally and in Asia and the Pacific. Initial hopes of a quick 2020 economic rebound are starting to fade, and it is increasingly likely that full economic recovery will take longer. The experiences of the 2008 financial crisis have demonstrated that the impact of an economic recession for a demand-driven sector, such as transport, can be felt for quite some time.

Just as transport has played a central role in the spread of COVID-19, it can be designed to play an important role in promoting a more sustainable transport mode balance through more active promotion of clean vehicles; provision of quality travel alternatives in public transit; and encouragement of active modes of transport, such as walking and cycling, to enhance overall health and well-being.

More sustainable design and construction methods, early warning systems, and disaster response plans need to be put in place to enhance governments' readiness to respond better to another disaster. More robust logistics and supply chains will be critical in enhancing countries' resilience to future shocks. Technological advances, big data, artificial intelligence, digitalization, automation, renewable sources of energy, and electric power can potentially offer fresh, innovative solutions to tackle changing needs, engendering smarter cities.

Governments need to work in partnership with the private sector to ensure there is an enabling regulatory and legislative environment to facilitate innovation. Increasing demands from governments and citizens for greater involvement call for a more user-centered approach in the design and delivery of transport services.

Far from covering all details needed for future transport planning, this guidance note has aimed to assess the impacts of COVID-19 on the transport sector in Asia and to guide policy makers in ADB DMCs and the ADB transport community on how best to respond to this unprecedented crisis.

More research is needed to understand what needs to be put in place to enhance the preparedness and agility of transport systems to tackle another pandemic or natural disaster. Further studies are recommended in the short term to (i) explore alternative measures to mitigate operational and financial impacts on public transit and aviation, (ii) collect emerging evidence on changing consumer behavior and travel patterns, (iii) develop plausible future scenarios and strategies to guide the planning and development of transport projects, and (iv) strengthen policy dialogue and technical assistance to support the DMCs.

In the medium term, it is recommended to step up efforts to promote sustainable transport projects to counter the negative trend of a possible shift to private modes by (i) further promoting public transit, (ii) providing quality alternatives in active transport modes such as walking and cycling, (iii) promoting e-vehicles, and (iv) developing green infrastructure delivery approaches. Transport system resilience could be enhanced by better harnessing advanced technology and promoting digital inclusion. Preparedness for multiple simultaneous hazards and disasters could be mainstreamed in project design to promote enhanced pandemic and disaster resilience.

Our actions today will affect our built environment and quality of life for decades to come.

Appendix 1
Timeline of Restrictions on Transport and Mobility

January—June 2020

Date	Event
AUSTRALIA	
20 March	International borders closed to all noncitizens and nonresidents
20 March	State and territory borders begin closing, beginning with Tasmania
15 May	New South Wales relaxes lockdown, allowing public gatherings
AZERBAIJAN	
28 February	Border with Iran closed
14 March	Land and air borders with Turkey closed
	Public transportation banned to limit interregional and intercity travel
22 June	Borders remain closed to passenger traffic
	No flights into or out of the country
BANGLADESH	
14 March	All flights from European countries stopped, with the United Kingdom the sole exception
23 March	Public transport limited as a safe-distancing measure
31 May	Lockdown fully lifted after previous weeks of easing
BHUTAN	
06 March	Restricted entry of all foreign tourists
13 April	Border with India closed on Indian initiative
22 June	Border restrictions on travelers remain
BRUNEI DARUSSALAM	
15 March	Departures from country suspended
	Mass gatherings banned but no known travel restrictions
24 March	All foreign visitors and foreign transit banned
26 June	Flights operated by Royal Brunei Airlines remain limited to a few countries
CAMBODIA	
13 March	Cruise ships entering via Mekong River banned
18 March	Thailand unilaterally closes border with Cambodia
22 March	All borders closed with exception of Poipet–Aranyaprathet, which allows trucks and trade
08 April	Travel across provinces and between districts outside the capital of Phnom Penh restricted
30 June	Expected end of lockdown and reopening of borders
GEORGIA	
16 March	Entry of all foreign nationals banned
20 March	Air travel suspended
14 April	Lockdown of country's four largest cities—Tbilisi, Kutaisi, Batumi, and Rustavi
	Entry and exit restricted, but movement within city still possible outside curfew hours
	Railway traffic suspended except technical transportation
	International and local freight transportation suspended
11 May	Lockdown in Tbilisi lifted
15 June	Domestic tourism restarts

continued on next page

Appendix 1 *continued*

Date	Event
INDIA	
09 March	Land border with Myanmar closed
13 March	All passenger traffic from all neighboring countries, except Pakistan, halted
16 March	Passenger traffic from Pakistan halted
24 March	Nationwide lockdown instituted
	All transport services—air, rail, road—suspended
08 June	National lockdown eased
INDONESIA	
20 March	Jakarta limits public transportation hours from 6 a.m. to 8 p.m.
26 March	All access, inbound and outbound, from West Papua is suspended
27 March	Tegal, Central Java implements local lockdown, prevents entry or exit from the city
04 April	Jakarta bans motorcycle taxis
31 May	Lockdown eased in limited territories
08 June	Lockdown eased in Jakarta
JAPAN	
03 April	Effective entry ban on international travelers
07 April	State of emergency declared for Tokyo and select prefectures
16 April	State of emergency extended countrywide
	No known domestic travel restrictions
25 May	State of emergency lifted across all of Japan after weeks of relaxation
27 May	International travel ban (for identified countries) redefined, but ban continues for majority of countries
KAZAKHSTAN	
29 January	Passenger buses and trains to and from the People's Republic of China (PRC) suspended, air traffic regulated
15 March	Entry and exit to country via all means of transport restricted, except for diplomatic services
19 March	Nur-Sultan and Almaty quarantined, entry and exit restricted
22 March	Nur-Sultan and Almaty rail and air services blocked, rail services continue
11 May	National lockdown eased
01 June	Railway transport and bus routes restart
LAO PEOPLE'S DEMOCRATIC REPUBLIC	
30 March	All passenger transport suspended
01 April	Last international flights depart
	Travel between provinces restricted
18 May	Internal travel fully reopens after weeks of easing
MALAYSIA	
16 March	Movement control order imposed nationwide
	International travelers restricted from entry, domestic travel limited
16 April	Ban on interstate travel announced for Ramadan period
09 June	Lockdown lifted, country enters phased recovery
MONGOLIA	
24 February	Travel between provinces banned, public transport suspended
10 March	Intercity passenger transport services including domestic flights and travel by private vehicle to Ulaanbaatar suspended
	Most international flights banned
30 June	Expected end of "advanced emergency readiness"
	Flights to resume 1 July

continued on next page

Appendix 1 *continued*

Date	Event
MYANMAR	
(Date unclear)	All flights to Myanmar suspended until 30 April
15 April	Borders with Bangladesh, India, Lao People's Democratic Republic, PRC, and Thailand closed
16 May	Restrictions eased in major cities, Mandalay and Yangon
NEPAL	
16 March	Patna (Bihar, India)–Nepal bus services suspended
20 March	All international flights suspended
24 March	Nationwide lockdown begins, public transport suspended
15 June	Lockdown eased, but nighttime curfew imposed; no pedestrian or vehicle travel between 10 p.m. and 5 a.m.
NEW ZEALAND	
19 March	Borders closed to all but New Zealand citizens and residents
25 March	National lockdown instituted
	Self-isolation rules limit all domestic travel and interactions
11 May	Phase out of lockdown begins (11–21 May)
08 June	Country declares virus eliminated
	International travel restrictions remain
	No domestic travel restrictions
PAPUA NEW GUINEA	
30 January	All travelers from Asian countries banned
	Border with Indonesia closed
16 April	Public transportation banned as national capital district goes under lockdown
16 June	State of emergency lapses
	International flights and border crossings remain banned
PEOPLE'S REPUBLIC OF CHINA[a]	
23 January	Transport in Ezhou, Huanggang, and Wuhan suspended, closing public transport, buses, railways, flights, and ferry services
	Departures from Wuhan airport still allowed
14 March	Mobility controls lifted in areas outside Wuhan
08 April	Lockdown fully lifted, all transportation resumes
PHILIPPINES	
15 March	Land travel (including all means of public transportation), domestic air, and domestic sea travel in and out of Metro Manila suspended
16 March	Travel restrictions expand to encompass all of island of Luzon
01 June	Restrictions eased in Metro Manila after weeks of countrywide easing
	Local carriers resume domestic flights
08 June	Limited international flights allowed to resume
REPUBLIC OF KOREA	
04 February	Ban on entry of all foreigners traveling from Hubei Province, PRC
29 February	Social distancing guidelines released
08 April	Extensive international travel restrictions imposed
06 May	Social distancing greatly relaxed (entertainment venues reopen)
SINGAPORE	
31 January	Ban on all new visitors with recent travel history from mainland PRC
25 February	Ban on all visitors from Cheongdo and Daegu, Republic of Korea
22 March	Ban on all short-term visitors arriving or transiting through Singapore
03 April	"Circuit breaker" begins, restricting public gatherings
01 June	"Circuit breaker" ends

continued on next page

Appendix 1 *continued*

Date	Event
03 June	"Fast lanes" implemented—limited flights to select PRC cities resume allowing business travelers subject to strict health testing
SRI LANKA	
19 March	Ban on all aircraft landing at Bandaranaike International Airport
22 March	Ban on all incoming passenger ships and planes
12 May	National lockdown lifted
24 May	National lockdown reinstituted until 26 May
	Further extension of selective lockdown restrictions (focusing on gatherings, not specifically travel)
THAILAND	
26 March	Partial nationwide lockdown
	Travel between provinces limited
03 April	Evening curfew instituted, emergency services exempt
09 April	Full lockdown of Phuket—airport closed, land and sea entry points closed
01 June	Interprovincial travel allowed to resume but not encouraged
TIMOR-LESTE	
19 March	Border closed with Indonesia
26 May	National lockdown lifted
UZBEKISTAN	
28 February	Land border with Kazakhstan closed (unilaterally by Kazakhstan)
21 March	Public transport operations halted
04 June	National restrictions eased
22 June	Limited lockdown in select districts of Tashkent
VANUATU	
26 March	Borders and airports closed
30 March	Interisland travel banned
April	Banned entry of foreign aid workers intending to assist with Cyclone Harold relief operations
VIET NAM	
22 March	Entry of all foreigners suspended
25 March	All Vietnamese carriers suspend international routes
01 April	Public transport services within major cities (Ha Noi and Ho Chi Minh City) suspended; domestic flights and passenger trains continue to run on limited service
20 May	Travel ban lifted for limited countries
22 June	Border with Cambodia reopens

[a] As the epicenter of the pandemic, response in the PRC was widespread. This charts only major events in Hubei Province.
Sources: The Humanitarian Data Exchange (HDX). COVID-19 Global Travel Restrictions and Airline Information (accessed 23 April 2020); and Aura Vision. Global Covid-19 Lockdown Tracker (accessed 26 June 2020).

Appendix 2
Changes in Visits to Public Transport Stations

15 February–14 June 2020

Afghanistan

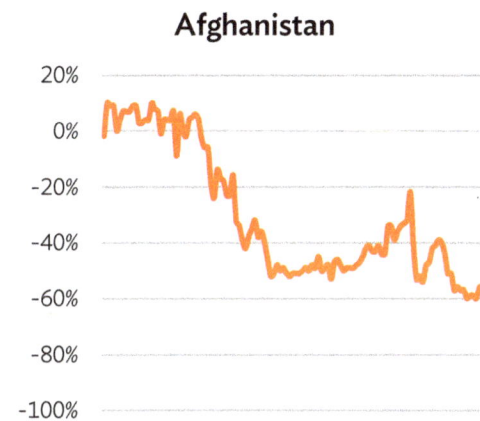

Australia

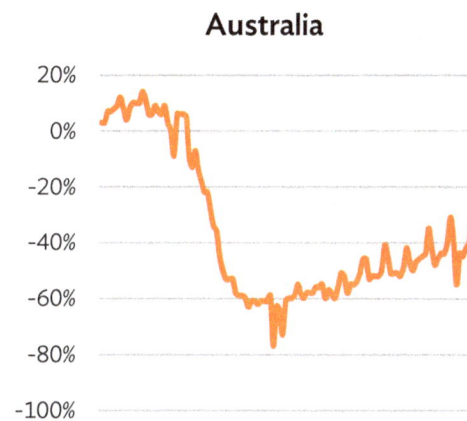

Bangladesh

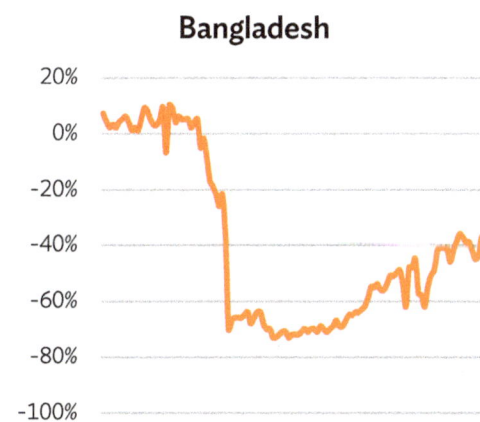

Cambodia

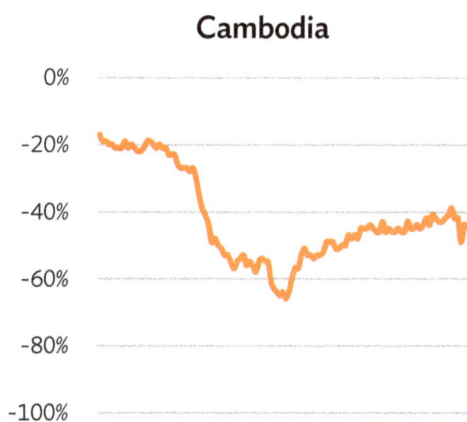

Fiji

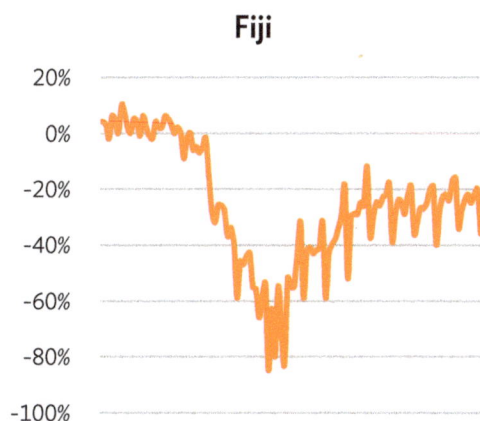

Georgia

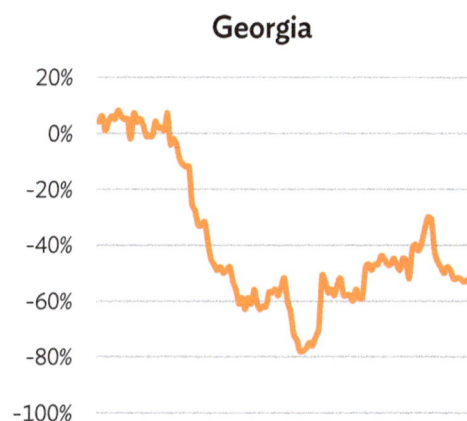

continued on next page

Hong Kong, China

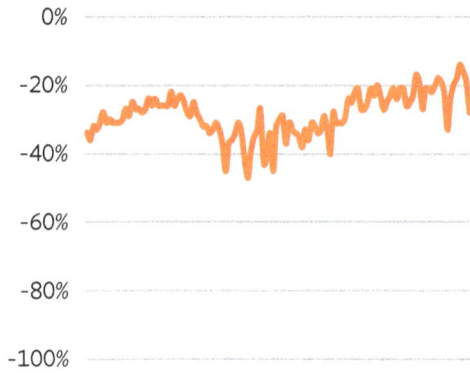

India

Indonesia

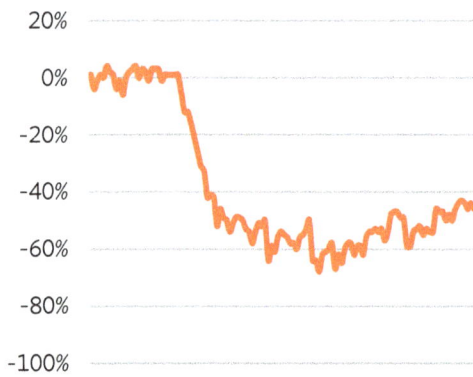

Japan

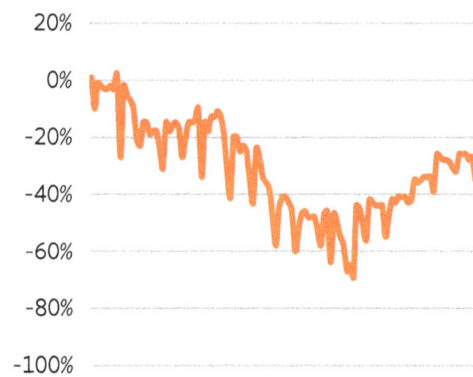

Kazakhstan

Republic of Korea

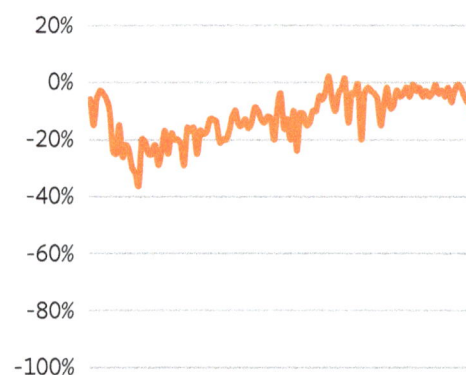

continued on next page

Kyrgyzstan

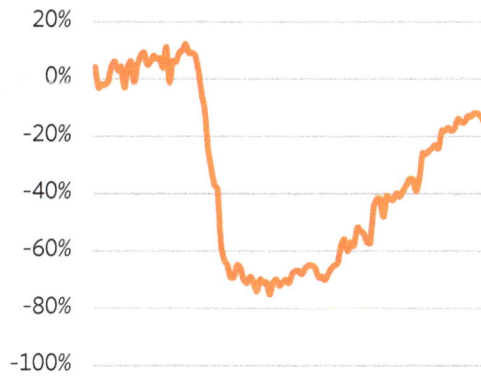

Lao People's Democratic Republic

Malaysia

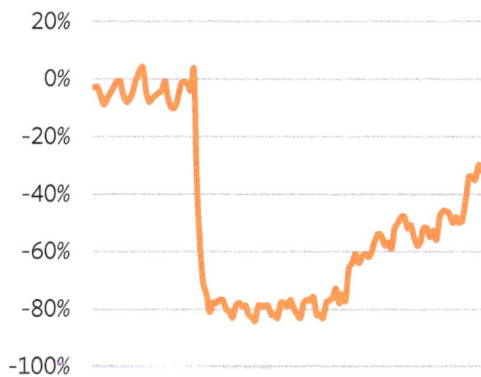

Mongolia

Myanmar

Nepal

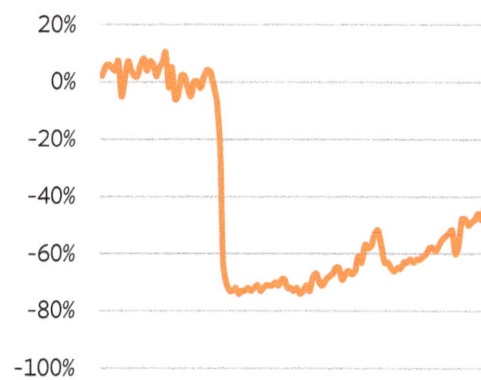

continued on next page

New Zealand

Pakistan

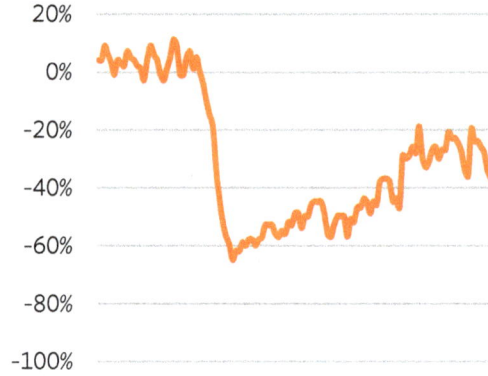

Philippines

Singapore

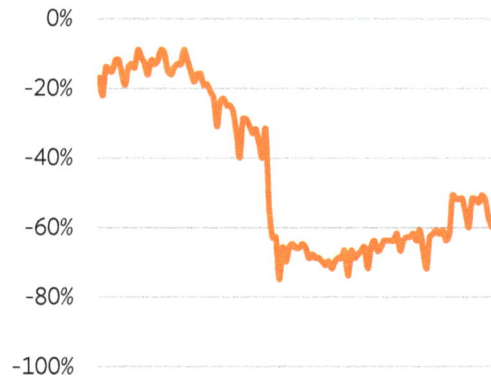

Sri Lanka

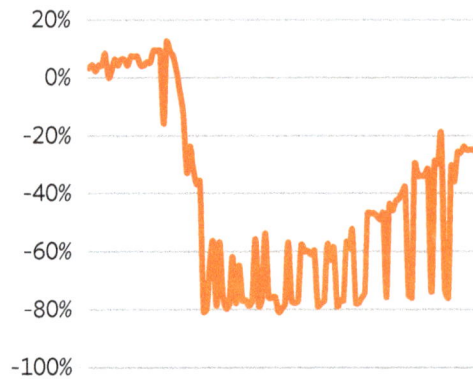

Taipei,China

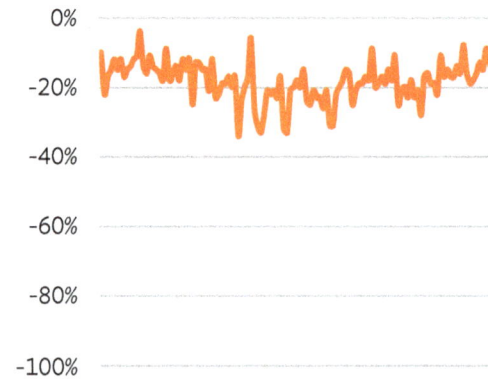

continued on next page

Appendix 2 *continued*

Tajikistan

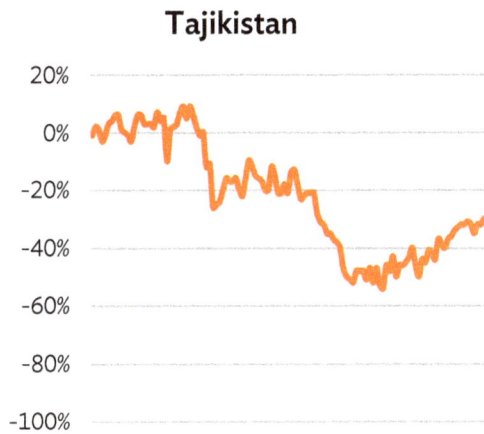

Thailand

Viet Nam

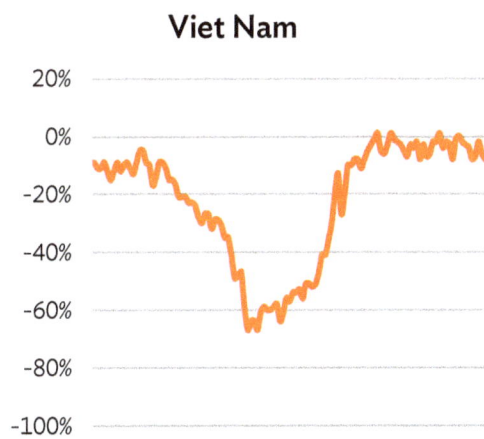

ADB members (average)

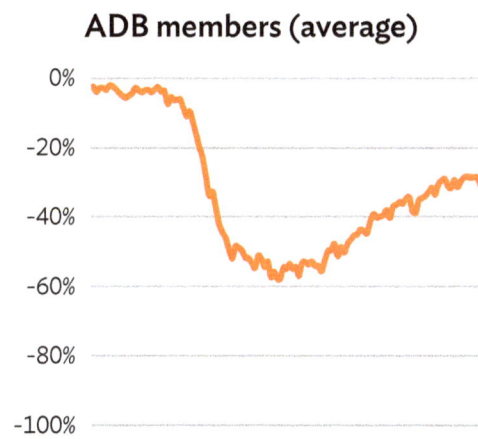

ADB = Asian Development Bank.
Source: Google. COVID-19 Community Mobility Reports (accessed 24 June 2020).

Comparison of Transport Trends in ADB Members

India

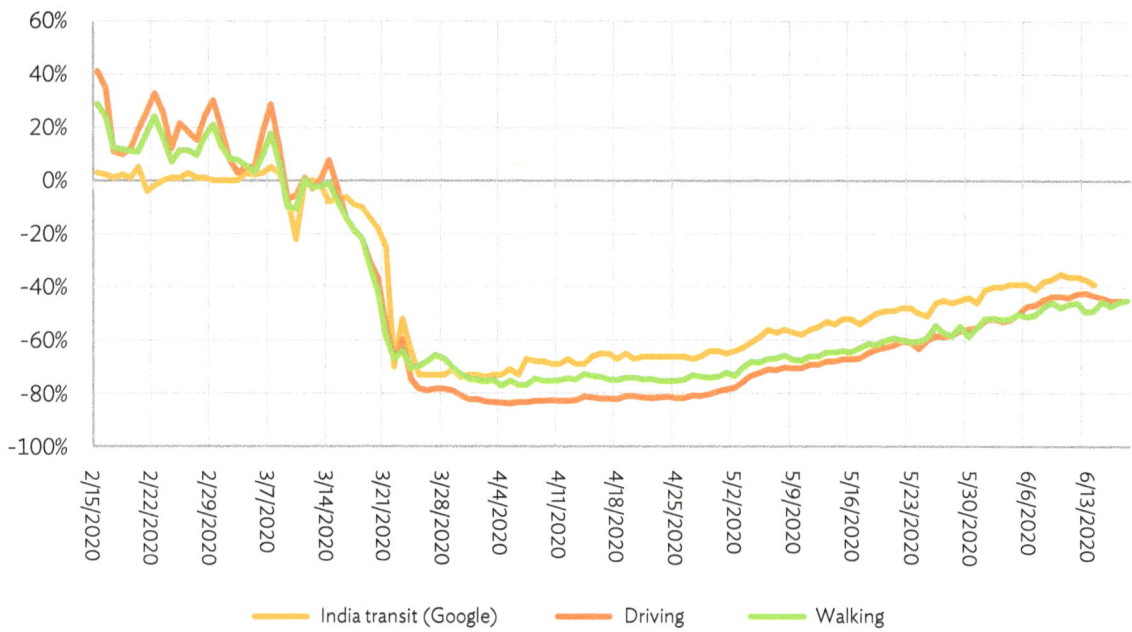

Legend: India transit (Google) — Driving — Walking

Japan

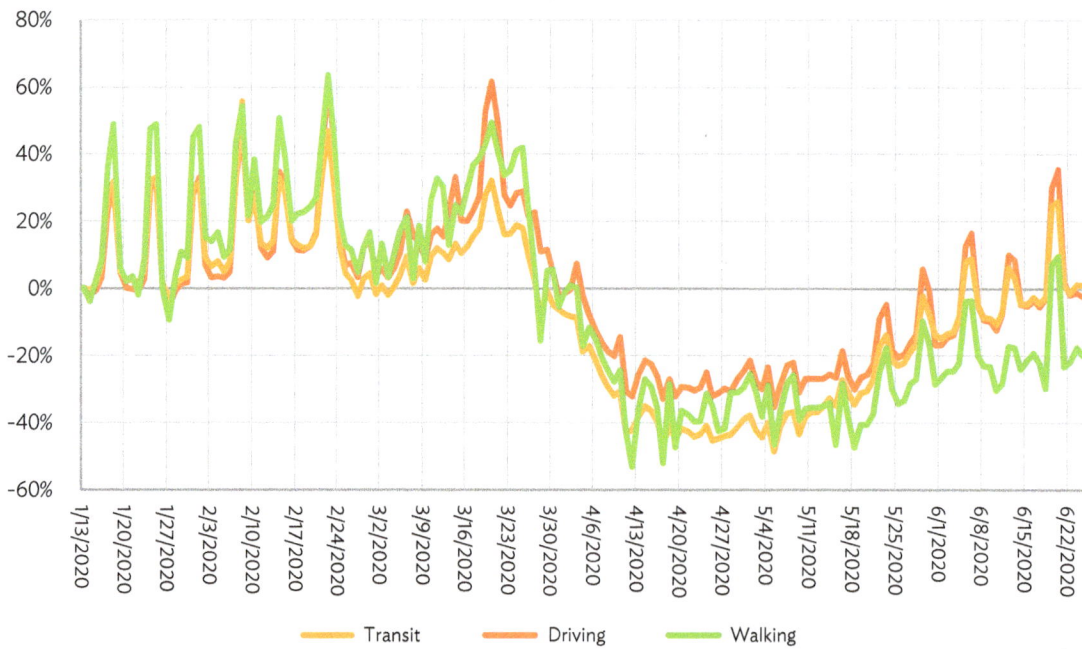

Legend: Transit — Driving — Walking

continued on next page

Appendix 3 *continued*

Philippines

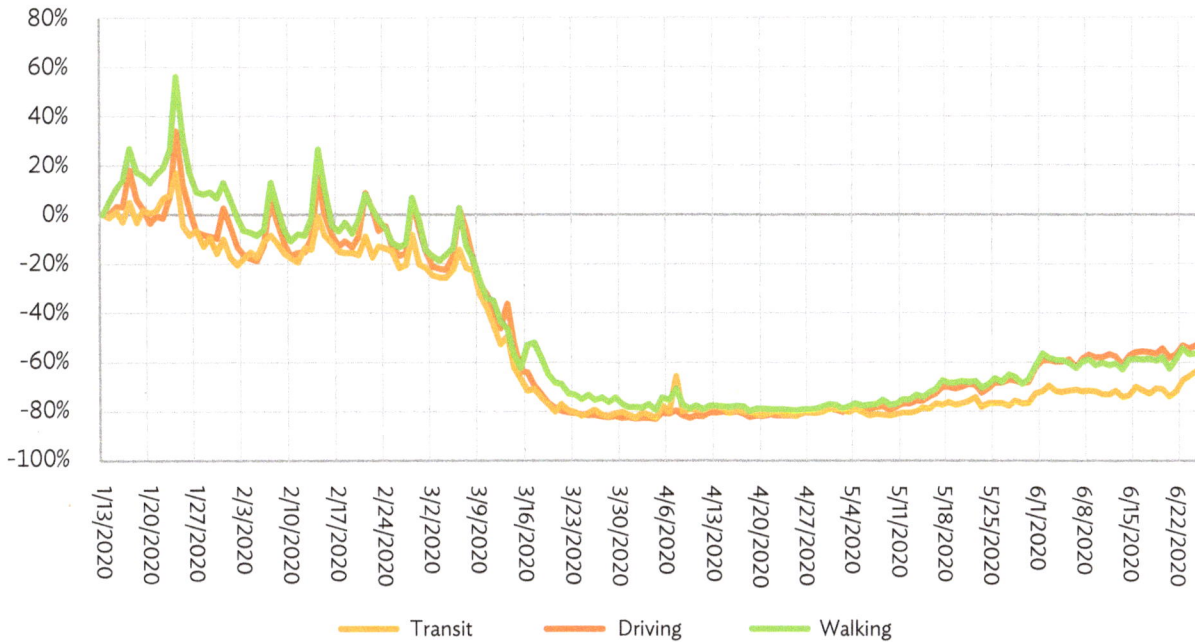

Transit   Driving   Walking

Singapore

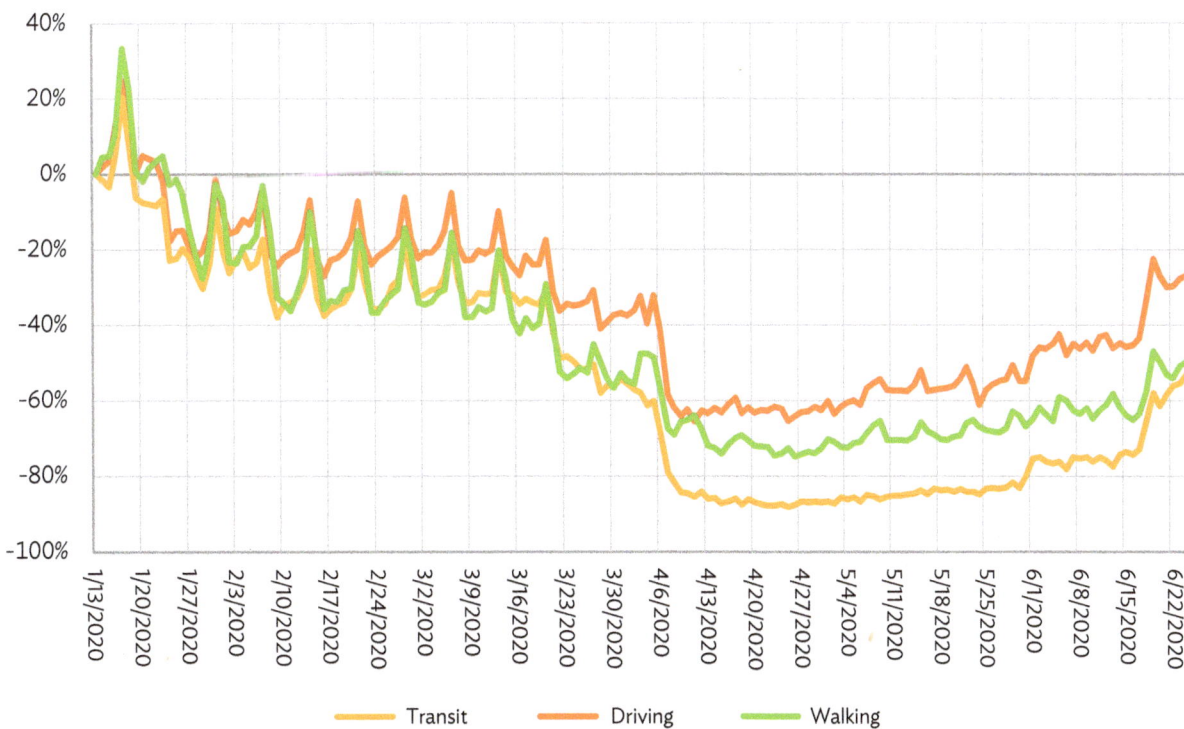

Transit   Driving   Walking

continued on next page

Appendix 3 *continued*

Taipei,China

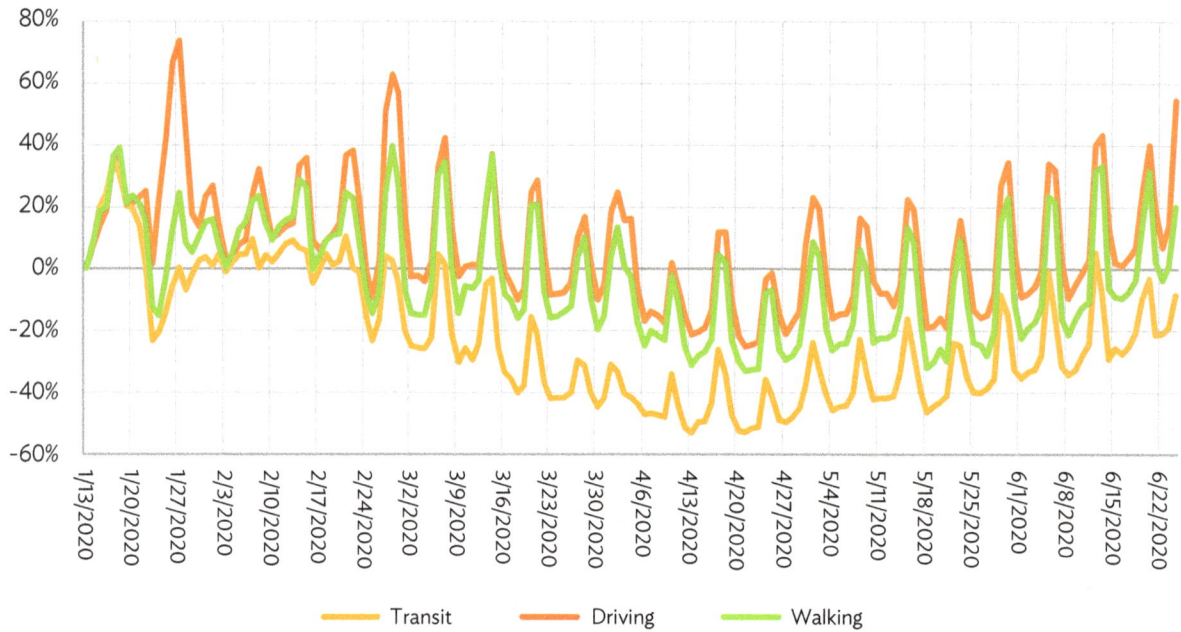

Thailand

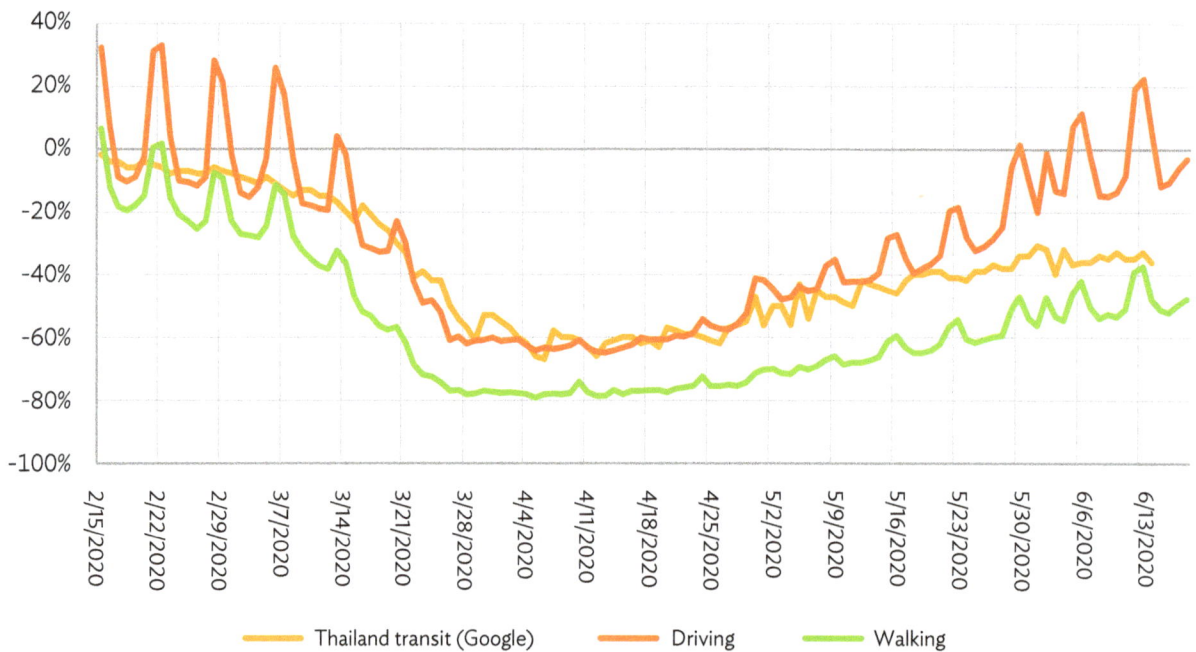

ADB = Asian Development Bank.
Sources: Apple, Inc. Mobility Trends Reports (accessed 24 June 2020); and Google. COVID-19 Community Mobility Reports (accessed 24 June 2020).

Appendix 4
Detailed Measures for Each Subsector

Enabling Condition Prior to Reopening
Response — Contact tracing.
Put in place a reliable health monitoring system to track rate of infection.
Supply adequate protective equipment for all staff and passengers, e.g., masks and disinfectants.

Public Transport

Response	For new mass transit projects, develop pandemic and disaster preparedness and response plan comprising early warning systems and pandemic and crisis management plan.
	For existing public transport systems, develop pandemic operations plan comprising protection of staff and passengers, and infrastructure. Protect staff through training, provision of timely information, provision of protective gear, and preventive health checks. Protect infrastructure through more frequent cleaning and disinfections. Protect passengers by requiring wearing of masks during travel, reconfiguring public transport for safe distancing, and conducting health screening at access points. Incorporate physical barriers or distance between passengers and drivers and customer service staff. These could be Plexiglass or temporary barriers using tape. Put in place health and contact tracing measures.
	Restructure concession and service agreements or financial subsidies for public transport operators.
	Implement demand management measures. Use advanced seat booking on public transport. Make transport demand-responsive to cope with crowd levels on fleets. Promote work practices to limit number of staff in offices (e.g., work-from-home and staggered shifts).
	Flexibly deploy transport resources to deliver priority services, e.g., use trains as hospital facilities and disinfected chartered buses and taxis to transport essential workers, if needed. Flexibly deploy transport resources to support growing demand in urban logistics, e.g., taxis to meet surge in demand for last-mile deliveries. Develop platform services, if absent, for the delivery of food and essential goods.
	Avoid physical interaction between passengers and driver by requiring advance ticket purchase prior to boarding.
	Contact tracing may be introduced on public transport through readily available mobile phone applications using QR codes (i.e., recording passengers' movement on public transport system).
Recovery	Use contactless payment, potentially integrated with contact tracing capabilities.
	Implement demand management measures. Monitor crowd levels in real time on public transport so operators can adjust service frequencies to proactively reduce passenger crowding.
	Review and improve reconfiguration of passenger flows, balancing safe distancing and efficiency.
	Explore balanced solution with stepped-up preventive health measures (e.g., only healthy persons travel, robust protection of passengers to relax safe-distancing requirement).

continued on next page

Appendix 4 *continued*

Public Transport

Recovery	Conduct health screening (e.g., only healthy passengers travel, health symptoms are checked at access points).
	Review risk allocation structure of concession and service agreements to enable public transport operators to stay viable. Explore short-term service contracts with chartered service operators.
	Provide bridging loans to assist operators with cash flows and credit lines.
	Promote flexible use of underutilized public transport capacity to meet shortfalls in health services (e.g., empty trains used as temporary health facility, taxis transport essential workers).
Rejuvenation	Mainstream contactless payments in public transport fares ticketing system, with opportunity for integration with other e-payment systems.
	Share data between public and private players to provide a foundation to develop mobility as a service and artificial intelligence in public transport (which bring together public transport and private sector ride-sharing and bike-sharing on one platform).
	Prepare pandemic-resilient transport plan for the future outbreak for (i) public transport, (ii) taxi and hailing service, and (iii) e-commerce and delivery system.
	Develop financing structures for adjusted service plan catering to reduced demand post lockdown.

Active Transport (Walking and Cycling)

Recovery	Develop and scale up walking and cycling capacity by reallocating existing road space.
	Allocate road space to walking and cycling zones only, particularly in commercial or tourism areas.
	Provide financial support especially for small and medium-sized enterprise transport operators, and formal and informal paratransit.
	Promote cycling through school advocacy campaigns and subsidized purchase costs and bike repairs.
	Utilize appropriate walking and cycling as well as paratransit vehicles, which are lower density services, to supplement public transport services, where necessary.
	Enhance road safety through physical and nonphysical measures to protect pedestrians and cyclists.
Rejuvenation	Develop guidelines and city agency capacity for pop-up bicycle lanes and emergency lanes in future pandemic and disaster operations plan.
	Develop city active transport masterplan to increase network infrastructure, support new micromodes, and implement strong advocacy campaign to promote a walking and cycling culture as a viable alternative to other modes.
	Share data between public and private players to provide a foundation to develop mobility as a service and artificial intelligence in public transport (which brings together public transport and private sector ride-sharing and bike-sharing on one platform).

Roads

Response	For new road projects: Develop pandemic and disaster preparedness and response plan comprising early warning systems and preparation of pandemic and crisis management plan. This can include flexible reallocation of road space for mixed-use traffic (fast and slow-moving modes such as nonmotorized transport). Put in place hard and soft measures to allow emergency responses in future by, for example, converting some lanes to emergency lanes that allow essential workers and first responders.
	Restrict travel in private vehicles to essential workers and other allowed travelers. Do not allow travel across state, province, and/or city boundaries into areas with substantially higher COVID-19 impact.

continued on next page

Appendix 4 *continued*

Roads

Recovery	Implement "slow streets" or walking and cycling lanes (maximum speed limit of 20–30 kilometers per hour) to enhance road safety for walking and nonmotorized transport modes.
	Adjust street design to reallocate road space to allow additional space for walking and cycling.
	For new roads and existing critical (high-volume) roads, implement road safety measures on urban roads and critical national and rural roads to protect vulnerable users.
	As types of nonessential travel are relaxed, slowly expand allowed travel distance from home.
Rejuvenation	Amend road design standards to allow for increased allocation of road width for walking and cycling.
	For existing road network, improve maintenance and operation of prioritizing improvement of unsafe road sections to three stars or better.
	Mainstream temporary traffic measures in road design standards to accommodate permanent or temporary increased capacity for walking and cycling, or emergency lane.
	Develop integrated masterplan (temporary measures) across modes as part of pandemic response and operations plan.

International Passenger Travel (Aviation)

Response	Develop pandemic operations plan, comprising protection of staff and passengers, and implementing safe-distancing measures. Protect staff through training, provision of timely information, provision of personal protective equipment, and preventive health checks. Protect infrastructure through more frequent disinfections. Protect passengers by requiring masks during travel, reconfiguration of public transport for safe distancing, and health screening at access points.
	Introduce "health passports" that require health screening to be introduced as far upstream as possible to minimize impact on operations at the airport, i.e., passengers arrive at the airport "ready to fly." Development and enforcement of this concept requires coordination with relevant health and immigration authorities.
	Design passenger flow through all departure and arrival processes to ensure safe-distancing requirements are complied with.
	For international arrival, governments should consider electronic declaration options (mobile applications and QR codes) to minimize human-to-human contact. Deploy health monitoring applications to incoming passengers to facilitate strict enforcement of home quarantine orders.
	Flexibly deploy transport resources to deliver priority services, e.g., allow cabin crew to meet staffing shortfalls in health care.
Recovery	Introduce contactless processes wherever feasible. This could include baggage check-in and passport control processes. In particular, governments should remove any regulatory obstacles to enabling such things as mobile or home-printed boarding passes and electronic or home-printed baggage tags.
	The measures undertaken in the response phase should be monitored and reevaluated periodically. When more effective, suitable, less disruptive, and scientifically supported measures become available, they should be implemented at the earliest opportunity to replace more burdensome and less effective old measures.
	Although reliable rapid testing is not yet available, the use of testing might be considered an additional preventive measure in the multilayered approach. In particular, if medical testing reliability improves, this measure can be used to remove other upstream measures.
	Establish a regional cooperation body to coordinate travel restrictions across borders (promotion of "travel bubbles").

continued on next page

Appendix 4 *continued*

International Passenger Travel (Aviation)

Rejuvenation	Develop contactless processes and systems for embarking and disembarking processes.
	Given the absence of confirmed evidence that people who have recovered from COVID-19 and have antibodies are protected from a second infection, immunity passports are not a mature measure now. However, if supported by scientific evidence, they can further facilitate the resumption of air travel as many of the protective steps can be bypassed.
	For remote countries, governments may consider various institutional reforms to the aviation sector. Relaxation on ownership requirements and local aviation regulations, as well as flexible public–private partnership arrangements, can help ensure the required connectivity.

Urban Logistics

Response	Contactless delivery should be more widely practiced, particularly for small parcel and last-mile delivery services. Electronic payment for goods can be made in advance, and the driver can leave the goods on the doorstep and communicate with the customers remotely via a mobile phone application to provide the electronic delivery note with photos.
	Nonmotorized transport and paratransit mode users could be deployed to fulfill shortages in last-mile delivery services.

Freight and Logistics (Air, Maritime, and Urban)

Response	Enhance disinfection and sanitization regime of goods, wherever relevant, and of property and facilities.
	For local delivery, governments should help logistics service providers overcome the challenges of obtaining sanitary equipment (e.g., masks) and recruiting enough staff.
Recovery	To make up the lost belly cargo space on passenger flights, governments should remove the regulatory obstacles and speed up the approval process for special charters, repurposing passenger planes for cargo operations, and relaxing crew quarantine requirements.
	Governments may consider chartering special flights for time-sensitive export goods to ensure cargo space availability and to prevent surged cargo rates for exporters.
	Establish a regional cooperation body to coordinate travel restrictions across borders.
	Introduce the "green lanes" concept. Dedicated freights lanes can be established to streamline cross-border movement of goods.
	Contactless delivery should be more widely practiced, particularly for small parcel and last-mile delivery services. Electronic payment for the goods can be made in advance; the driver can leave the goods on the doorstep and communicate with the customers via a mobile phone application to provide the electronic delivery note with photos.
	Probably as part of a bailout program, governments may consider working with airlines to ensure minimum scheduled services or regular charters to keep the lifeline of the local economy uninterrupted.
	Restart the supply chain and repair any broken links. Stockpile and replenish materials.
Rejuvenation	Governments can support and facilitate the deployment of nonmotorized transport and paratransit to fulfill shortages in last-mile delivery services.
	Governments can support technology development to boost delivery efficiency, based on smooth flows of funds and information. However, when embracing the concepts of digital platforms and the sharing economy, extra attention should be paid to the adverse impact of operators' natural monopoly status, such as price manipulation and reduced employee welfare.

COVID-19 = coronavirus disease.
Source: Asian Development Bank.

Appendix 5
Useful Guidelines and References

Public Transport

- International Association of Public Transport. 2020. *Management of COVID-19: Guidelines for Public Transport Operators.* February. https://www.uitp.org/publications/management-of-covid-19-guidelines-for-public-transport-operators/

- International Association of Public Transport. Articles and resources on responses by public transport operation operators in tackling COVID-19. https://www.uitp.org/news/coronavirus-outbreak-uitp-and-public-transport-sector.

- Transformative Urban Mobility Initiative. Fighting Corona in Transport. Corona Transport Knowledge Platform. https://www.transformative-mobility.org/corona.

- International Road Transport Union. Coronavirus (COVID-19) Information Hub. https://www.iru.org/covid19.

- Transportation Research Board. A collection of online resources on COVID-19 impact on transport. https://www.nationalacademies.org/trb/transportation-research-board.

- American Public Transportation Association. COVID-19 Resource Hub. https://www.apta.com/.

- S. Ibold, N. Medimorec, and A. Wagner. 2020. The COVID-19 Outbreak and Implications to Sustainable Urban Mobility. *Sustainable Transport in China.* 13 March. https://www.sustainabletransport.org/archives/7653.

Nonmotorized Transport

- MOBYCON. 2020. *Making Safe Space for Cycling in 10 Days: A Guide to Temporary Bike Lanes from Berlin.* Delft. https://mobycon.com/updates/a-guide-to-temporary-bike-lanes-from-berlin/.

- London Cycling Campaign. 2020. Back on the Bike? Top Tips for Cycling during the Coronavirus Crisis. *Cycling Advice.* https://lcc.org.uk/pages/cycling-advice-2020?.

- Institute for Transportation & Development Policy. 2020. As the Impacts of Coronavirus Grow, Micromobility Fills in the Gaps. *Transport Matters Blog.* 24 March. https://www.itdp.org/2020/03/24/as-the-impacts-of-coronavirus-grow-micromobility-fills-in-the-gaps/.

- Institute for Transportation & Development Policy. 2020. Five Temporary COVID Measures that US Cities Should Make Permanent. *Transport Matters Blog.* 13 April. https://www.itdp.org/2020/04/13/five-temporary-covid-measures-that-us-cities-should-make-permanent/.

- International Transport Forum. 2020. Re-Spacing Our Cities for Resilience. *COVID-19 Transport Brief.* 3 May. https://www.itf-oecd.org/sites/default/files/respacing-cities-resilience-covid-19.pdf.

- A. Schwedhelm, W. Li, L. Harms, and C. Adriazola-Steil. 2020. Biking Provides a Critical Lifeline During the Coronavirus Crisis. *World Resources Institute.* 17 April. https://www.wri.org/blog/2020/04/coronavirus-biking-critical-in-cities.

- United Kingdom Department for Transport. 2020. Statutory Guidance—Traffic Management Act 2004: Network Management in Response to COVID-19. 23 May. https://www.gov.uk/government/publications/reallocating-road-space-in-response-to-covid-19-statutory-guidance-for-local-authorities/traffic-management-act-2004-network-management-in-response-to-covid-19.

- *BBC News*. 2020. Coronavirus: France Offers Subsidy to Tempt Lockdown Cyclists. 30 April. https://www.bbc.com/news/world-europe-52483684.

Aviation

- World Health Organization. 2020. Operational Considerations for Managing COVID-19 Cases or Outbreak in Aviation: Interim Guidance. 18 March. https://apps.who.int/iris/handle/10665/331488.

- International Air Transport Association (IATA). 2020. *Biosecurity for Air Transport: A Roadmap for Restarting Aviation*. https://www.iata.org/contentassets/4cb32e19ff544df590f3b70179551013/roadmap-safely-restarting-aviation.pdf.

- IATA. 2020. *Guidance for Cabin Operations During and Post Pandemic*. Edition 3. 5 June. https://www.iata.org/contentassets/df216feeb8bb4d52a3e16befe9671033/iata-guidance-cabin-operations-during-post-pandemic.pdf.

- Airports Council International. Industry Information on COVID-19. https://aci.aero/about-aci/priorities/health/covid-19/.

- International Civil Aviation Organization. Collaborative Arrangement for the Prevention and Management of Public Health Events in Civil Aviation. http://www.capsca.org/.

- IATA TravelCentre. COVID-19 Travel Regulations Map. (Summary of travel restrictions and quarantine requirements by country). https://www.iatatravelcentre.com/international-travel-document-news/1580226297.htm.

- Singapore is establishing "green lanes" with countries with low transmission rates. "For a green lane arrangement to work, both countries would have to first have confidence in each other's safeguards and be able to coordinate their quarantine orders so that travelers might only need to be tested or quarantined once." See T. Goh. 2020. Singapore in Discussions with S. Korea, Australia, to Establish "Green Lanes" for Travel. *The Straits Times*. 30 May. https://www.straitstimes.com/singapore/transport/singapore-in-discussions-with-s-korea-australia-to-establish-green-lanes-for.

- European countries are easing travel restrictions. See A. Wilson. 2020. Which European Countries Are Easing Travel Restrictions? *The Guardian*. 19 June. https://www.theguardian.com/travel/2020/may/18/europe-holidays-which-european-countries-are-easing-coronavirus-travel-restrictions-lockdown-measures.

- International Civil Aviation Organization. Council Aviation Recovery Task Force Take-Off Guidance. Guidance for Air Travel through the COVID-19 Public Health Crisis. https://www.icao.int/covid/cart/Pages/CART-Take-off.aspx.

Cross-Border Freight and Logistics

- European Commission. 2020. *COVID-19 Guidelines for Border Management Measures to Protect Health and Ensure the Availability of Goods and Essential Services*. Brussels. 16 March. https://ec.europa.eu/home-affairs/sites/homeaffairs/files/what-we-do/policies/european-agenda-migration/20200316_covid-19-guidelines-for-border-management.pdf.